FROM ME TO WE

A Guide for Community Stewards

Eva Jo Meyers
Arika Virapongse

From Me to We: A Guide for Community Stewards
By Eva Jo Meyers and Arika Virapongse

Published by Spark Decks. Printed in the United States of America.

Cover and text design by Danijela Mijailović
Cover artwork by Eva Jo Meyers

Tradepaper ISBN: 978-1-949298-26-0

First Edition, December 2025

While every precaution has been taken in the preparation of this book, the publisher and author assume no responsibility for errors or omissions, or for damages resulting from the use of information contained herein.

Table of Contents

List of Tables and Figures

Introduction

When I was in 8th grade, some friends and I formed an "environmental club" we called SOS (Save Our Soil). We led such a successful trash-a-thon picking up garbage off the side of the road, we didn't know what to do with all of the cash we raised.

My memories of our club are vague, but we did have appointed positions like secretary and treasurer. We held meetings and events, created flyers, and wrote letters to leaders to fight for the environment. We were organized, active, and we were making a difference.

Without specific know-how or a theoretical frame-work, I realize now that what had started as a loose group of like-minded friends evolved into an empowered and impactful community of purpose. It's a pattern I have seen repeated around me dozens of times, whether by design or happen-stance, at my kids' school, in my workplace, or online. It is amazing what can be done when a group has some goals, a bit of coordination, and the desire to make a difference. —Eva

We wrote this guide because we believe that communities are an essential part of a thriving human existence, for the following three reasons:

Communities increase connection. It's in our human nature to crave connection, and communities are one of the most important ways that we organize ourselves in society to bring connection into our lives. According to a 2023 Meta-Gallup survey[1], a quarter of adults across the world feel lonely, and this loneliness epidemic is literally killing us. Lack of connection to each other is tied to depression, illness, and overall poor physical health. Recognizing this, some medical providers now prescribe community and connection as a way to overcome our chronic loneliness.[2]

Communities amplify empowerment and impact. Communities are an effective mechanism to get things done, inspire improvements, and fight for what we believe in. A community's impact can extend far beyond its immediate surroundings or membership, creating feedback loops and ripple effects that galvanize further community building and lasting change. While an individual can certainly have an impact, this effort is amplified when a group of people works together[3].

Communities help us generate holistic solutions. Humanity's increasingly complex needs and built environment have generated thorny problems, like climate change, widening income disparity, and global health crises. Solving these issues requires cross-disciplinary approaches that draw on the collective wisdom and expertise that are impossible to find in a single individual[4]. Collaboration in the form of well-run communities creates an opportunity for solutions that would be impossible to imagine or

---

[1] Meta and Gallup (2023) The Global State of Social Connections. Gallup Inc. www.gallup.com/analytics/509675/state-of-social-connections.aspx.

[2] Murthy, VH (2020) *Together: The Healing Power of Human Connection in a Sometimes Lonely World.* HarperCollins Publishers, New York, NY.

[3] National Academies of Sciences, Engineering, and Medicine (2025) *The Science and Practice of Team Science.* Washington, DC: The National Academies Press. https://doi.org/10.17226/29043.

[4] Hou, X, R Li, and Z Song (2022) A Bibliometric Analysis of Wicked Problems: From Single Discipline to Transdisciplinarity. *Fudan Journal of Humanities and Social Sciences* 15(3):299–329. doi: 10.1007/s40647-022-00346-w. Epub 2022 Apr 6. PMCID: PMC8985063.

implement without a diverse group representing a wide range of creativity, knowledge, and skill.

If you are reading this book, we're guessing that you, too, already understand the potential of community. You may also already know that building and sustaining them is a lot easier said than done. Most of us don't put a lot of thought into how to foster them, or notice how our communities are functioning at all—until there's a crisis or break-down.

What you'll find in these pages are strategies, best practices, and principles that you can use to cultivate inspired communities with ease and fun.

By helping you understand your community and your role as a Community Steward, you will be better able to support a meaningful entity that energizes everyone who joins.

Getting the resources and buy-in your community needs to feel sustained is also key. By building your confidence and improving how your community is stewarded, you'll also be able to make your pitch to funders, supervisors, colleagues, and friends about the importance of community building and the value they'll get out of being a part of your work.

Are you a Community Steward?

Any organization that cultivates or interacts with a community or external audience has a Community Steward. For many organizations, however, it's not very obvious who this person is. When I'm trying to identify the Community Steward in an organization, I might try asking people who holds titles like community manager or outreach specialist. Oftentimes, I'm told: We don't have anyone like that. So I'll attend meetings to observe who might be organizing things—even if they are in the background. Or, I'll ask employees which staff member interacts with external people the most. I'm always sure that if they've got a community, then they've got someone who's doing the work of organizing and supporting people who are a part of it. — Arika

It would be nice if people in a community could just organize themselves. But, the reality is that at least one person is needed to smooth out pathways for collaboration, and help independent activities stay harmonized and energized. This person (or persons) is a Community Steward.

To help you decide if you are a Community Steward (or want to be), we encourage you to reflect on the following characteristics.

There is no single title for a Community Steward. What makes someone a Community Steward is that they have taken on the responsibility of organizing and supporting a group of people to help them connect and work together. There are many different job titles where that responsibility may fall:

- (Community) Manager
- (Vice-) President
- Coach
- Lead
- Mayor/Political Leader
- Teacher
- Event-planner
- Principal
- Director
- Counselor
- Librarian
- Instructor
- Chief-of-Something
- Coordinator
- Organizer
- Religious Leader
- Advisor
- Administrator
- Communications specialist
- (add your own title here)

The bottom line? It's not your title that makes you a Community Steward. It's your role, goals, and actions that do that.

Community Stewards see where community is needed. A community might exist as an unnamed group of people or even as a yearning within an existing group that has yet to manifest. A Community Steward is the person who energizes the group to make community happen.

Take the public library, for instance. No longer just a quiet building that houses books, many public libraries today have become community centers. There are children's storytime (where you can meet other exhausted parents), coding and crochet clubs (a thin disguise for teens to hang out with others with similar interests), and computer classes (it feels good to know I'm not the only one who needs help learning new technology). Each library visitor, whether or not they hold a library card, is a member of that community. And the librarians? They are the Community Stewards of it all.

Community Stewards are connectors. Being a connector means that you are driven to pull the threads that help bring people together. You enjoy getting to know people, and connecting them with each other: "Oh, you should really meet my next door neighbor, she collects vinyl records too." You know that it's not about you, but about supporting the relationships of the people around you.

Community Stewards want to support improvements. As we were working on this book, Jaylen Smith was elected mayor of Earle, Arkansas. He was 18 years old—one of the youngest mayors in U.S. history. "I didn't run to make a name for myself," Smith told CNN after winning the election. "I ran because I wanted to help my community and move my community in the direction that it needed to be moved in."[5]

Do we believe an 18-year-old can be the Community Steward of a city? Absolutely. You do not need to have a specific degree, title, or years of experience to step into the role of Community Steward. What you need is to see an opportunity to bring people together to make your corner of the world a better place.

Community Stewards create systems that empower people. There is a fine line between *enabling* community members, and *empowering* them to do their work. Community Stewards often take on administrative work that supports people, but their bigger impact is on creating systems that communities can use to independently organize themselves and collaborate.

If you could see yourself in any of the characteristics described, chances are you're a Community Steward. Perhaps another community member or colleague also popped into your mind. The reality is that there may be more than one Community Steward in your community, and you may share these characteristics between yourselves.

How should I use this guide?

We have organized this guide into five sections. Our intention is that as you read this guide, you'll be able to focus on the areas of community steward-ship that you need most. You're encouraged to review the table of contents and start with what-ever stands out to you as being relevant to your needs at the moment. Let your enthusiasm for a topic lead you.

We suggest that you read this book while holding a specific community in your mind. The more specific you can be, the more you'll be able to reflect on your own experiences and learnings. In the next section, we invite you to Get Oriented, by offering tools to help you define and clarify the community you are thinking about.

In the spirit of "micro-practices," we encourage you to tackle one suggestion in the book at a time rather than trying to do everything you read about all at

---

[5] Mizelle, S (2022) Arkansas city elects 18-year-old to be next mayor. CNN. https://www.cnn.com/2022/12/07/politics/jaylen-smith-earle-arkansas-mayor/index.html.

once. A micro-practice means picking one small thing to try–one idea, one practice, one exercise–and sticking with that for a while before trying out another. If you can implement just one idea from this guide, that is success.

We recognize that many communities today leverage the online environment. A challenge with writing about online platforms is that these platforms change almost daily. When you come across an online infrastructure term (it will be capitalized) in this book, you can refer to Chapter 22 "Improve Your Virtual Infrastructure" where we have defined different categories of online tools.

We are truly glad you are here, and look forward to connecting with you in real time, off the page, or out in the communities we are all a part of.

NOTES

Get Oriented:
Look from Different Angles

Reflect on this: Knowing who you are is the first step towards becoming who you want to be.

Before we launch into filling you with ideas on how to build, strengthen, and sustain your community, we want to give you an opportunity to get more clear on what your community is and does. Like professional organizer Marie Kondo advises, let's dump out everything in our dresser drawers so we can see what we're dealing with[6]. Then we can figure out what to keep, what to cut, and what to build out further.

The assessments on the following pages are designed to help you answer these key questions:

1. What are the boundaries of your community?
2. What kind of community are you?
3. Where is your community right now?
4. Is your community empowered and impactful?

You can try out these assessments on your own, but they are best done with other community members who might have different perspectives to share. You can answer the questions together as a group or do the assessment individually, and then compare responses. You can make modifications to the assessments, too! Using the assessments in this way may spark some interesting discussions within your community.

There are many other assessments throughout the chapters in this guide. The ones you'll find here are just a starter set to help you take a look at the basic framing of your community from various view-points.

Please keep in mind that these assessments only offer a snapshot of your community. We encourage you to release any feelings of judgments that arise as you complete them. There are no right or wrong answers.

---

[6] Kondo, M (2014). *The life-changing magic of tidying: A simple, effective way to banish clutter forever*. Random House.

Assessment 1: What are the boundaries of your community?

Regardless of whether you've articulated it already or not, every community has some kind of outline or edges that defines what it is and does. Sometimes, these boundaries of a community are clear, and other times, they are vague.

Identify what holds your community together by considering three parameters:

- **Commonality**: What do people in your community all have in common? What makes someone a "member" of the community?

- **Purpose**: What does your group want to achieve together? Why do they want to be a part of the community? What might motivate someone to join the community?

- **Activities**: To be more than just a group of people, a community *does* things together. What are some of these activities?

Let's take people in a neighborhood (which is sometimes formalized into an Homeowners Association) as an example:

Table i. Parameters that make your group a community.

Commonality:		Purpose:		Activities that members do:
We live near each other within a bound geographic area.	+	We want to have a safe, pleasant, and supportive quality of life.	+	• Decide on neighborhood rules. • Organize potlucks. • Manage a community garden.

Now it's your turn! Table ii is a template that you can use to help determine the parameters of your community. Remember, this is a very high-level bird's eye view just to give you a rough outline.

Instructions:

1. Start by adding your Community Name and Today's Date you filled out the template.
2. Then, note what members have in common (Commonality), what people want to achieve together in the community (Purpose), and the activities that your community does (Activities).
3. Once you've filled in the table, return to the "Activities" column and make a note of the name of the person(s) who helps make each activity happen. These people are most likely the Community Stewards in your community.

Table ii. A template for identifying your community's commonality, purpose, and activities.

Community Name:		Today's Date:		
Commonality:	+	Purpose	+	Activities (Add the name of the person who helps make each activity happen):

Did anything new come to light as you completed the table? Do you feel more clear on what holds your community together?

Assessment 2: What Kind of Community Are You?

Being aware of the *kind* of community you are can help determine what strategies might work for your community. Most communities fall into at least one of five different types; take a look at the descriptions in Table iii below, and consider which type might best describe your community.

Many communities are a mixture of different types, and may function like one type or another depending on their needs. For example, your place-based community may decide to take some action, like a neighborhood clean up, and suddenly feel more like an action-based community.

Don't worry too much about putting your community exactly into these boxes. The point is to notice in general what kind of community you are, so you can bring more clarity as to why you exist.

Table iii. Some common types of communities.

	**Professional Communities.** These communities are organized around a shared profession. They can take the form of office colleagues, project teams, professional learning associations, consortia, and external audiences that a business or organization is seeking to engage with more. Purpose: To improve their professional practice, strengthen their influence in a sector or domain area, align their services to the needs of their clients or customers, and grow their profession sustainably by recruiting early career members.
	**Interest-based Communities.** These are communities connected to a shared interest, practice, or identity. Some examples are book clubs, spiritual/faith-based centers, meet-up groups, and recreational activity groups (e.g., tennis, gardening, crafting, pets). Purpose: To connect like-minded people, help members improve their skills and learn, have fun, and feel inspired and uplifted.
	**Action-based Communities.** These communities are dedicated to pushing forward change and progress. They include Parent-Teacher Associations, political action committees, nonprofit boards, advocacy groups, and unions. Purpose: To influence decision-making and systems change, create and maintain momentum around specific actions, and advocate for the interests of their community.
	**Cohort communities.** These are groups of learners who are recruited to come together for a specific time-limited purpose. Subsequent groups may be organized, and each group can be added to the existing one in order to grow the community. Examples include people who join a training or fellowship program, or obtaining an educational or professional degree. Purpose: To provide value for members by expanding their learning, and deepening and maintaining the impact of the cohort program's purpose.
	**Place-based communities**. These communities are groups of people who share local environmental resources, like land, forest, and water. The neighborhood where you live is one example, and each one of us is a part of a place-based community. Purpose: To coordinate efforts to manage, use, survive, and thrive on shared environmental resources.

Assessment 3: Where is your community right now?

It had been four months since my kids had last seen their grandparents. Visiting them really brought home how much they'd grown. "Oh wow!" their grandparents exclaimed when we walked in the door, "The kids have gotten enormous!" The four-month gap made the change in their height apparent in a way that I hadn't noticed in the day-to-day. And yes, they are taller than I am now. —Eva

As Community Stewards, we are often so close to a community we cannot see changes within it clearly. We may have a general sense of the direction things are heading in (it *seems* like we have more participation now), but without tracking it, we don't really know for sure.

Communities (like teenagers) can quickly change and evolve over time. Doing assessments once–or even twice–a year, and comparing the results of each assessment, can help you stay updated on how your community may be evolving. Such information can help you determine where you might need to do more work, for example, realizing that you need/can afford a paid staff member now that your membership has doubled.

In the assessment below (Table iv) are some common dimensions that you can use to measure your community. We'll refer to these dimensions throughout the book, so you might find it useful to identify them now.

Table iv. Dimensions of your community.

Today's Date:		
Dimension	**Description of Dimension and Question to Consider**	**Current Status in my Community**
Size	Do you consider your community to be small (less than 50 people), medium (50-250), or large (250+ people)? *If your community doesn't have formal membership, you can estimate.*	
Participation Levels	How often do members volunteer to do things in the community? How often do they interact with each other outside of events? Is it easy to get people to step into leadership positions?	
Human Resources	What is the balance between volunteers and paid staff? How much more support is needed?	
Criteria for Joining	Does your community allow anyone to join? If there are criteria for joining, what are those?	
Membership	What requirements must a member meet to maintain their membership? *Examples: Members might be required to volunteer a certain number of hours, participate in meetings, or live in a certain geographic area.*	
Governance	What documented operational structures do you have in place (e.g. voting, bylaws, policies)? Who makes decisions? How does someone become a decision-maker?	
Location	Is your community place-based, or online? What is the balance between these? *Examples: "Place-based" = in your town. "Online" = members live anywhere. "Balance" = online but most members live in the U.S.*	

Assessment 4: Is your community empowered and impactful?

> *Serendipity Books in the small town of Chelsea, Michigan was relocating their book store to just one block away. While the owner could have packed her 9,100 books into boxes and hired movers to get the job done, instead she chose to call upon her community to form a "book brigade."[7] About 300 people showed up, ranging from small children to the elderly. Each book was pulled out from its original location, and passed hand to hand through the line, until the very last person placed it on its new shelf. Each time a shelf was completed, a cheer went up in the crowd. Finally, the last book was shelved, and the community celebrated together for what they had all accomplished. — Arika*

In this guide, we want to support you in working towards a specific type of community—one that is empowered, impactful, and purposeful.

What does that mean? One way to understand what that looks like is to compare "an empowered and impactful community of purpose," with… the alternative. To give you a better sense of how to spot the difference, we've created a chart (Table v) that you can use to assess a community.

To use Table v, choose a community that you'd like to assess. Then go through each row, and circle or highlight which statement (A or B) best describes your community.

Please note that most communities will have a mixture of statements from both A or B columns. You may find elements of empowerment in groups that you might perceive as not empowered overall. Likewise, there is rarely a community that is fully empowered and impactful, with no room to grow. The purpose of this chart is to offer a framework to understand what we are working towards in this guide.

> We invite you to take some time to reflect on these questions after you complete the assessment:
>
> → Did anything surprise you as you completed the assessments? If so, what and why?
>
> → Which aspects of your community were hardest to determine or define? Do you feel like you need more information from your community?
>
> → How do you feel about the status of your community? What issues do you face? Is there anything that you'd hope to change in the future?

---

[7] Associated Press (2025) "Book brigade: US town forms human chain to move 9,100 books one-by-one". The Guardian (April 16) www.theguardian.com/us-news/2025/apr/17/book-brigade-us-town-forms-human-chain-to-move-9100-books-one-by-one

Table v. How an empowered and Impactful Community of Purpose is different from other communities.

Topic	1. Community that is NOT Empowered, Impactful, and/or Purposeful	B. Empowered and Impactful Community of Purpose
1. Belonging	People are not sure if they belong, and may not have strong ties to the group.	Members feel that they belong and feel strong ties to the group. They often praise, promote and invite others to join.
2. Idea sharing	Members hesitate to share their ideas for fear that they won't be taken seriously, or will be shut down, or simply because they don't know how or who to share those ideas with.	Members readily share their ideas, and feel confident that not only that these ideas are valued, but that they will be uplifted by the group. Members don't feel afraid to say unpopular things.
3. Community Value	Members are unsure of the value of the group.	Members consistently find value in participating, and seek out opportunities to do so.
4. Expertise sharing	Members do not have opportunities to share their expertise.	There are systems in place for members to share their expertise with each other.
5. Leadership	There is not an obvious path for members to take on responsibilities or roles within the community, and volunteering is limited to a handful of active members.	There is a system in place for members to step into (and out of) leadership and other roles within the community; a broad constituency of members often volunteer to help out.
6. Membership diversity	Membership (and especially leadership) tends to be homogeneous, consisting of people who look, think, and/or act like each other.	Membership (and especially leadership) is diverse and includes a broad range of perspectives, social identities, and backgrounds.
7. Documentation	Documentation is disorganized, and it can be difficult for members to access shared materials, meeting details, or calendars.	Documentation is organized and easy to access. Members can quickly find the materials or meeting details they are looking for.
8. Awareness	Members are not aware of everything going on within the community, and often feel themselves caught off-guard by announcements.	Members are generally aware of what is going on in the community, and don't feel surprised by important announcements.
9. Decision-making	Decisions that affect the entire community are made by a handful of active members and/or leadership. It is often unclear how decisions are made and by whom.	The majority of members participates in decision-making that affects the entire community; the process is clear and everyone who wants to weigh in can.
10. Financial transparency	There are ongoing disagreements or discontent over membership dues, finances, budgets, or resources, which may be controlled or hidden by one or two people in charge.	There is transparency around how finances work within the community; there is flexibility and input from members on how money is collected and spent and members feel in alignment with decisions.
11. Conflict management	Inter-member conflict and gossip are common, there may be factions within the community competing for power or resources; people may often feel forced to take sides.	Members feel there is a way to positively address conflict within the community, and trust that their wellbeing is considered when issues arise.

SECTION I
CULTIVATE YOUR MEMBERSHIP

Reflect on this: Your members are the heart of your community.
By tending to individuals, you nourish the community itself.

Building and maintaining your community's membership can be one of the most rewarding–and challenging–parts of being a Community Steward.

In this section we offer ideas for cultivating a healthy and connected membership, where people feel like they are a vital part of the group. It's often easiest to attend to members who have the resources to participate or automatically feel like they belong, but here, we hope to encourage you to also reach and engage the members who fall beyond that inner circle–people who may not yet be sure of the value of the community and their place within it.

Despite what we may like to believe, feeling a sense of belonging within a community is not something that just happens. It requires vigilant and constant effort, and is one of the most important elements of community stewardship. Without it, members feel ill at ease. Such members may be left wondering why they are there, and if it's worth their effort to continue trying to participate.

To see how belonging functions within your community, think of it as taking place on three levels:

1. Belonging amongst individual community members

If you have ever seen a group of ants fall into water, you may have seen how they cling together and create a raft. Likewise, connections that are forged between two or more individuals within your community can serve to keep those members afloat. A member does not need to be connected to everyone in the community, but being closely connected to at least a couple of other members is essential.

2. Belonging between a community and its leadership

Community leaders help tie a community together. They are people who members can go to when they need help, and especially if they are experiencing a conflict. Community Stewards are one such leader, so making sure that you are approachable and accessible helps members feel like they matter.

3. Belonging within the community as an entity

Cultivating relationships between an individual community member and the community as a whole requires an artful balance between the needs of the individual and the imperatives of the group. Such a concept has been referred to as a Nested-I[8], where "the individual achieves meaning and identity through the social context of communities and society—and society constitutes itself through the flourishing of the individual." On the one hand, a healthy community cannot be composed of individuals that do whatever they like at the expense of others. On the other hand, aggregating everyone into a faceless group also erases the unique diversity and individualism that makes communities so rich. This is the difference between valuing individuality over individualism.

---

[8] Bollier, D and S Helfrich (2019) *Free, Fair, and Alive*. https://freefairandalive.org/read-it/.

Most people don't come right out and say "I don't feel like I belong here." Instead, people vote with their feet and fade out. Part of being a great Community Steward is growing your capacity to carefully observe and listen between the lines, consistently keeping a watch on what you and your team can do to help all members feel welcomed and connected.

As you embark on this section, it may be helpful for you to think of instances in your life where you've felt a strong sense of connection and belonging within a community. What helped you reach that feeling? On the flip side, you may also want to reflect on times when you were part of a community where you didn't feel valued or connected. What led to those feelings for you? There is a lot to learn from your own experience, and even more to learn from the experience of others.

NOTES

CHAPTER 1
Support the Membership Journey

In a small group that I steward, on one or two occasions someone has shown up to a meeting who I could swear I had never met before. On one such encounter, I became truly worried. Had I forgotten this person somehow? Neither the name nor the face seemed at all familiar. Eventually, I found the courage to ask, "Remind me how you found your way to this meeting?" "Oh, my friend sent me the invite," they replied. I immediately found myself relaxing, relieved that I had not overlooked them, but that the community was valuable enough to someone that they invited a friend to join us. —Eva

As you are stewarding your community, one most basic tenet is so obvious that we sometimes forget it exists: Each person is on their own membership journey. A healthy community has a natural flow of people arriving, getting more or less involved, returning after time away, and possibly moving on completely to contribute to the life of yet another community.

To make this membership journey easier to address, we have broken it down into four stages. As you read the list below, see if you can identify a specific person in your community who is at each of the stages.

1. **Prospective members** are those who haven't yet joined but are interested. Maybe they've visited your website, or dropped by an event.

2. **New members** have just joined. They're in, but are still getting to know their way around. They may still feel unsure of whether or not they belong, and what benefits they may get out of investing in the community.

3. **Experienced members** have been around for enough time to feel like they understand how things work. They often have a deeper sense of commitment and belonging than new members do. Like the roots of a tree, experienced members often provide stability and direction for growth in the community.

4. **Past members** may be gone, but they are not forgotten. In some communities, they may have been so foundational that they are still considered members long after they are no longer part of the group.

A healthy community will have a good distribution of members across all four stages, although the more experienced members you have, the more stability your community will likely have.

One of your roles as a Community Steward is to make it easier for members to advance between stages. Here, we offer some suggestions for how to support members at each stage.

1. Prospective members

Help prospective members learn more about the community by creating ways for them to experience the community culture, get to know other members, and understand what it means to be a member.

❑ **Open a door.** Many people are rightfully hesitant about joining a new community. They want to know what they are getting into before they make a commitment.

To help prospective members to get to know the community, you could offer a trial period on an online community platform, or host a recurring open house event. Whichever trial activity you choose, make it easy for prospective members to join and allow them to participate passively–without strings attached. Focus on giving people the opportunity to get a sense of the community culture, ask questions, and talk one-to-one with existing community members.

❑ **Be transparent and explicit about what it means to be a member.** Most prospective members will want to know what is the purpose of the community, what are the benefits of joining, how one joins, and what is expected of members. The best way to make this information evident is to put it in writing–it can be on a social media page preview, a website, or an email that is shared with prospective members who register for one of your open public events. You can also designate a committee whose role it is to meet with prospective members to answer these types of questions.

❑ **Joining the community.** There are generally three ways a person becomes a member of a community:

→ **By invitation:** If your community is invite-only, it means you have a filter with which to select members. This could look like an application, a list of criteria, or other forms of gate-keeping that helps your community and a potential applicant decide if they are a good candidate for membership.

In this type of community, both members and Community Stewards are usually very well aware of who is part of the community, because joining took effort or action from both sides.

→ **By member choice:** In some communities, we do not select or curate who becomes a part of the community. With this model, membership is simply open to anyone who wants to join. People pay a fee, add themselves to a mailing list, or attend an event and they're in. In other words, people self-select to join the community, because they find that the community mission, goals, activities, and composition of members align with what they are looking for.

In this type of community, Community Stewards may or may not be aware of who has joined, and sometimes members may need support learning how the community works.

→ **By circumstance:** In this instance, people become members because they stepped into the boundaries of your community, sometimes without even realizing it. They may sign up for a library card, begin attending the school you teach at, or accept a job offer at your company, and just like that, they are now part of the community. In some ways, you could say that these people opted to be part of this community, but they may not even realize what they signed up for.

In this type of community, members will often need to be made aware that the community exists, how they "joined", and what it means to be a part of it.

Take a moment to think about which of the models above most accurately describes the community you are stewarding. What does it take for someone to "step into" your community and become a member?

2. New members

This stage focuses on helping new members feel welcomed, building their trust in the community, and giving them the resources they need to feel ready to jump in.

❑ **Send a welcome note.** As soon as the new member joins the community, give them something in writing, like an email, stating that they are now a member. Offer some basic first steps that they can take to get started in the community. Make sure you set things up behind the scenes so they can fully participate, for example, by adding them to internal online communication platforms and your mailing list.

❑ **Acknowledge their membership.** Peer acceptance is a key part of how someone shapes their identity within a community.[9] If you have a public-facing platform like a membership directory or webpage, add new members to it. You can also let the community know that a new member has joined, such as by announcing a batch of new members on your social media platforms or via your newsletter. If your group has swag or other materials, make sure new members receive those items.

❑ **Give members time to warm up.** New members often need time to get settled in. Make sure involvement options for members are clear, then give members time, space, and opportunities to figure out how (and if) they want to engage.

❑ **Send out regular communications.** New members will need a little help getting into the habit of thinking about the community, and consistent communication is the best tool for this. In these communications, you can reinforce the culture and tone of the community, as well as announce events and opportunities for members. Regular communications are often presented as a community newsletter or email, but it could also be a weekly or monthly post on Social Media or a Collaborative Workspaces.

3. Experienced members

Supporting experienced members is often about valuing the experience and knowledge that they have of the community and cultivating their leadership.

❑ **Create specific roles for experienced members.** Roles could be one-off activities like providing feedback on documents or hosting an event, or longer term roles like editing blog posts. Some roles can be done asynchronously (whenever people have spare time), and others can require synchronous participation like attending meetings. The point is to create opportunities for them to step up.

❑ **Provide the opportunity for mentorship.** Experienced members often feel confident within the community, so they are a great fit for helping recruit prospective members or helping newer members navigate the community. Whether it's partnering on planning an event, attending a workshop together, or just meeting up for coffee and a chat, we encourage you to invite your veteran members into the process of supporting newer members.[10]

❑ **Aim for leadership.** Experienced members are some of the best thought leaders and collaborators that you can have in your community. Create leadership roles and opportunities that experienced members can take on, such as by serving on Boards, and as committee chairs and working group leads. In addition to their leadership, keep an eye out for ways that their interpretations, ideas, and advice can get integrated into the underlying fabric of the community. When an experienced member steps up and expresses that they want to be involved, you'll want to make sure that you have different ways to say Yes.

---

[9] Individuals often feel empowered to act autonomously within a community space when they have attained peer acceptance. For example, see: Laudel, G and J Gläser, J (2008) From apprentice to colleague: The metamorphosis of Early Career Researchers. *Higher Education* 55, 387–406. https://doi.org/10.1007/s10734-007-9063-7.

[10] This phenomenon is also known as "legitimate peripheral participation", which is about how new community members lean on experienced members to become more proficient members in the community. See: Lave, J., and E Wenger (2001). Legitimate peripheral participation in communities of practice. In *Supporting lifelong learning* (pp. 121-136). Routledge.

4. Past Members

Just as you thoughtfully welcome prospective members to get a feel of your group and join you, putting effort into "off-boarding" members is equally as important.

❑ **Solicit their feedback.** Understanding why community members are leaving the community is an opportunity for you to learn more about your members. Exit interviews, surveys, or simply informally asking for feedback are all possible ways of gathering this type of useful information.

❑ **Acknowledge their exit**. As you did for prospective members, make sure you send something in writing to the member that confirms their exit from the community. Members can be encouraged to say their own goodbyes to the community through online community platforms, such as a community-wide post on a Collaborative Workspace. If a member is stepping back from a formal role in the community, you will want to announce this organizational change to the broader community, including who members should reach out to in the future. Note that leaving a formal role is different from announcing that the member is leaving the community, which is a private decision that should not be shared without their permission.

❑ **Offer ways to stay in touch.** Adding past members to a newsletter mailing list or social media page appropriate for "alumni" of your community can help them stay in the loop, even after they have formally stepped away. Contact lists or other document access might be something you'd like to offer as permanent resources to people who are no longer official members, but who still want to be connected.

❑ **Keep the door open**. Since people's lives change all the time, members may decide to come back in the future. If you host open non-member events, like a conference, you may see them showing up. In some ways, past members are like prospective members, so keeping the door open helps set the tone that they are always welcome.

As a Community Steward, being mindful of what stage people are in on their membership journey can help you better support their experiences in the community. You may even find it beneficial to share this model with your community, so they can see for themselves where they are, and be their own guide through the stages.

NOTES

CHAPTER 2
Shift Your Thinking Around Participation

A few years ago we planted milkweed in our front yard. Swarms of monarch caterpillars hatch on them each fall. Every year, the plants get devoured, far too small to sustain all of the larvae. So, I take a few of the caterpillars inside to place them into a special net we have. I gather more milkweed leaves, and fill the enclosure with food. We then watch with fascination as they gobble up the leaves and form chrysalises. Then comes the waiting. I check on them everyday: Will today be the day that they hatch? It is a miracle every time we put each young butterfly outside, knowing that they'll be back again next year to lay their own eggs on our milkweed plants. —Eva

Over months and years, you will undoubtedly notice that members float in and out of your community. A member might have a strong presence for months at a stretch, and then suddenly–like the monarch butterflies–you hardly see them at all.

These rhythms of presence can be reflected on a small scale. Some members may respond to emails immediately, while others may not get back to you for several days.

Such ebbs of participation can also be true for you as a Community Steward. At some points in your stewardship career, you may be present for every meeting and contribute to all important decisions. At other times, you might not be available in that way, and your community might feel confused by your absence, or even resentful.

We are guessing that you have experienced these types of rhythmic misalignment; when our rhythm, or a rhythm we have grown accustomed to, is disrupted by someone else marching to a different drummer. Sometimes the misalignment is so acute it causes conflict and distress.

Rather than viewing this inconsistency with alarm, here are some suggestions for how to embrace it.

❑ **Get to know the cycles that members are operating on.** Our human lives go through cycles that are influenced by our natural environment, biology, and social constructs.

Such cycles often take precedence over other things in life, because they may be related to people's essential needs[11]. A first step in getting into better rhythmic alignment is to ask your community (through conversations, surveys, or intake forms) which cycles influence them, so you can better anticipate the cadence of the community.

---

[11] Consider the well-known, but still debated, theory called Maslow's Hierarchy of Needs that broadly describes how people typically meet their basic physiological needs before they attend to more emotional needs.

Cycles to consider:

→ The standard work day and work week, e.g., the 9am to 5pm work day, night shifts, or week days versus the weekend.

→ Seasons of the year.

→ Academic year, such as fall, spring, and summer semesters, and school breaks.

→ Annual holidays, which can be religious, national, and regional.

→ Household life cycle[12], which includes when people are young and single, partnered with children, or retired.

→ Career stages, like early/late career, full time/part time workers, or on leave/unemployed.

→ Fiscal year for business, which is when accounts begin and close for tax and auditing purposes.

❑ **Use your data.** When you've been stewarding a community for a while, you might start to notice some patterns. For example, you might have less participation from members during the summer and holidays or a rush of new members when the school year begins, or notice that people often don't open emails sent on Fridays.

As with finding out about general cycles influencing your members, understanding what your data is telling you can help you make decisions like:

→ How often does communication material come out and at what time of day?

→ When do you send out an annual members' survey and how long is it?

→ When should people expect a big community event to happen?

→ How often does volunteer leadership turn over?

→ When should recurring meetings be scheduled and how frequently?

❑ **Mix things up.** There is no way to find a time or rhythm that will work for everyone, so at some point, you're just going to have to commit to something. When you do that, be aware that you could unintentionally create a feedback loop. For example, the people who are in attendance at a meeting are more likely to choose a meeting time that works best for them–and not others. This same issue occurs with the location of a meeting, the spoken/written language you use, and the communication channel you access.

How to get around this? Whenever you can, mix things up. Use multiple communication channels for the same important message, ask community members to make phone calls to members who don't text, or send important announcements via physical mail versus only in emails. If it's a very important meeting, hold the meeting at least twice so you can bridge time zones.

Having asynchronous ways of participation, like using an online collaborative document or recording a big event or meeting so people can watch it afterwards, is also great failsafe to help people stay involved.

While you can meet the majority of the group's needs through the points listed above, there will still always be members who are operating on a different rhythm that may simply not align with what is working for everyone else. With limited human resources, it can be overwhelming to try to make things work for everyone. Some people will fade in and out of the community no matter what you do.

Similarly, you may need to let go of your assumptions around what "good" participation and "good" membership looks like. If you find yourself feeling frustrated with a specific aspect of the participation of your membership, it may be time to re-examine your membership framing and strategy altogether.

---

[12] Also known as the "family life cycle", this is a sequence of stages that characterizes the formation, growth, and dissolution of family households.

In Table 2.1, take a look at how we often characterize "good" participation. Do any of these assumptions ring true for you? As much as we might wish that all of our members might behave in these ways, it's simply unrealistic for most people in a community.

Table 2.1. Common ways that participation and "good" participation in a community are often defined, and some ideas to shift your thinking around these assumptions.

Participation dimension	What this looks like	Assumptions of "good" participation	How to shift your thinking
Time	How much time a member puts into the community.	Lots of time	Instead of quantity, look at the quality of that time. Maybe a member only shows up for an hour of your event, but during that time they contribute valuable ideas or make people laugh. If a specific time commitment is being required of members before joining, you may be limiting who is participating.
Frequency	How often a member participates, such as the number of meetings or events the member attends.	All or most meetings	If you feel let down by how often people show up, maybe you need to reduce the number of meetings, or reconsider whether you are asking people to do too many things. Instead of measuring the success of your activities based on the number of people that show up, consider it a success if a different mixture of people show up each time.
Money	Whether or not they paid their membership dues or donate to the community.	Generously and on time	Consider all of the contributions a member brings to the community, including those that are nonmonetary. A member's activities can increase the value of the community, so that other people are now more likely to pay for it. Similarly, you may need to try a sliding membership fee[13] or other types of fee structures.
Interaction	The number of people any given member connects with and the quality of those interactions.	Many people and always positive	Not everyone is an extrovert, although we tend to build our world—and our standards—around this type of personality. As Susan Cain points out in her book, Quiet, "introverts tend to work independently, and solitude can be a catalyst to innovation."[14] What if we step away from tracking how profusely and exuberantly a member connects with other members, and look instead at how deeply they participate? Or if they are participating at all, regardless of whether it is highly interactive.

---

[13] A sliding membership fee is often determined based on someone's socioeconomic, political, and/or geographic circumstances.
[14] Cain, S (2012) *Quiet: The Power of Introverts in a World that Can't Stop Talking.* Page 74

Participation dimension	What this looks like	Assumptions of "good" participation	How to shift your thinking
Enthusiasm	How quickly a member jumps up to volunteer or how forcefully they say, "Yes!".	Quickly and forcefully	We tend to value the person who quickly comes to the rescue and pitches in, instead of recognizing that some people need time to think before jumping in with both feet. Learning to value, and make opportunities for, both types of participation can help everyone's level of participation feel equally worthy and beneficial.
Attention	How a member responds to emails, Social Media posts, and other communication from community organizers.	Attentively and enthusiastically	Adjust what you consider a reasonable amount of attention, and you may find yourself surprised by the fact that it wasn't the amount of attention, but the pace of attention that was disappointing you.
Promotion	If the member openly promotes the community and their affiliation with the community.	Always and often	There may be many reasons why a member does not actively promote the community, including those that are unassociated with how much value they find in the community. This is again an instance where you may need to adjust your expectations and try to see things through their eyes.
Activity	If the member engages in an activity within the community, either as a volunteer or participant.	Very actively in numerous activities	It can be exhausting to feel like people aren't pulling their weight. If you do feel this way about your members, it may be helpful to explore whether you are asking for too much from your community.
Service	If the member provides a needed service to the community.	For free and generously	Once again, here is an opportunity to let people decide when, how, and where they feel moved to serve. If none of your members step up to volunteer into an essential role in the community, you'll probably need to consider hiring someone to do that job.

While this chapter encourages you to be flexible, we also want to acknowledge that there is a balance between being inclusive of different types of participation, and being clear about what your community expects of members. It's not fair to anyone to say "We have no expectations," because that is likely not true. Plus, people thrive when they know where the boundaries lie.

To steward effectively, there's no way around acknowledging that participation comes in all shapes and sizes. So we ask you: In what ways can you expand and stretch your vision of participation and become more comfortable with ebbs and flows?

CHAPTER 3
Make Connections

We've lived in the same place for over ten years, and one of my favorite parts about that is all of the people we now know. We chat with neighbors when we are gardening outside. We meet friends when we run errands around town. We say yes to all the organized events that our kids' educational programs put on. It gives us the opportunity to talk with people we might have seen in passing, or meet completely new people we now realize we have a lot in common with. As our relationships deepen, so does our own feeling of belonging within the community. —Arika

A common challenge that Community Stewards face is isolation. By holding the responsibility of looking after the group as a whole, we might unintentionally hold ourselves (above and) apart from everyone else. Unfortunately, this separation makes it harder for members to develop trust with leadership, and by proxy, with the community.

Likewise, helping community members get to know each other, dissolves feelings of isolation and strengthens their trust and bonds with the community. According to social network theory,[15] a network with a mixture of both weak ties (greater degrees of separation between people) and strong ties (strong relationships between people) is most useful for helping people access resources and opportunities.

As a Community Steward, you can tend to both the weak and strong ties that a person has in a community as you help them make, navigate, and maintain their connections in the community. How do you know if you are doing it right? You start hearing about people working together or achieving successes together, and you had no idea that it was going on. Like the roots of a tree, these invisible connections are what creates a strong foundation for your community.

Below we share ideas to give you some inspiration on how to increase connection. Keep in mind that the goal is to break down any barriers between yourself and community members, and between members, so pick the ideas that seem like they will best help you accomplish those two goals.

☐ **Host regular new members meetings.** We suggest having a regularly scheduled open public event where anyone can attend, learn more about the community, and meet other prospective, new, and established community members. This event can double as both a first introduction to the community, and an orientation as to how the community works. This is an event that seasoned community members might enjoy hosting so that you can simply attend as a community member yourself.

---

[15] Aral, S (2016). The future of weak ties. *American Journal of Sociology,* 121(6), 1931-1939.

❑ **Make introductions.** You'll need to be knowledgeable enough about the community to be able to identify "bridging" opportunities for members. Stay on the lookout for members who share interests and goals–especially for members who are new to the community–and mention them to each other. You can directly broker a relationship between them, but ask for permission first since direct introductions can sometimes be a burden on people.

❑ **Support self-connecting.** Hosting a membership directory with people's contact information and information about what each person does so people can figure out who is in the community and who might share common interests with them can support people getting to know each other better. Directories can often have different levels of privacy, ranging from public (on a website) to restricted (for community members only) to private (for administration only). The best way to have a comprehensive directory is to make it part of the onboarding process, so a member has the option to be added to the directory when they join.

❑ **Schedule small-group talk time.** Host an "office hours" on a recurring basis when you'll be available to talk with anyone who'd like to chat. You can structure the time with brief introductions, Q & A, or even have a theme-of-the-month. If more than one person shows up at the same time, then you've created an opportunity for other members to get to know each other.

❑ **Showcase members.** Having ways to spotlight members is a wonderful way for people to broadcast their areas of expertise and interests, so other members can connect with them more easily. Some ways to do this include:

→ **Lightning talks.** Members are given a set amount of time for short 5-minute presentations to introduce themselves and share their contact information. These can be done in person at events, or asynchronously via videos hosted on a shared site.

→ **Blog posts.** Members can write from their personal perspective about a topic of interest and include information about how to get in touch with them.

→ **Spotlight in a newsletter.** If you've got a regular newsletter, you can feature a different member in each one. Ask them to answer standard questions and include a fun photo of themselves. You'll probably find it to be one of the most popular sections in the newsletter.

❑ **Participate.** To get a feel for how connection is (or isn't happening), spend time just *being* a member of the community. During meetings or events, look around and try to notice which community members might be feeling disconnected at that moment, and notice how you, yourself, are feeling. Taking an intentional look at connectivity by putting yourself in the shoes of community members can be a very eye-opening experience.

Remember that your goal is to have authentic relationships with members so that you don't become siloed, and to help members build relationships with each other so they feel connected to the community as a whole. As you read through this chapter, did anything shift in your thinking about the relationships you have with community members, or their relationships to each other?

CHAPTER 4
Notice Who's Missing

I recently attended a networking event where a quick visual scan revealed the attendees were mostly white women somewhere between 40 - 70, with very few men, young people, or people of color. I fit the majority demographic, but the noticeable homogeneity made me feel distrustful of the group that had coordinated the event because it was out of line with the demographics of the area where we live and work. What had their advertising been? Was this homogeneity intentional? Did anyone else notice this? —Eva

After reading Eva's story above, you may now already be thinking: Do the demographics of your community accurately represent the demographics of the population you are intending to serve? And if not, why not?

It is a rare community that doesn't suffer from some exclusion in the membership. More than likely, the groups that you'll find missing are those that have been historically marginalized, such as those with different ability status, race, gender, socioeconomic class, and ethnicity.

You might be missing dominant groups too. For example, where are all the men in our community that aims to tackle inequity in the workforce? Is this problem really going to get solved without them at the table?

This type of omission can also happen in sub-groups or committees within your community. For example, does one type of demographic do all the heavy lifting by planning and implementing events, while another demographic just enjoys the fruits of the labor by showing up to speak at these events?

A fully representative membership (and leadership) improves the impact of your community. Many of the issues that our communities are tackling require expertise, experience, and perspective from the broadest range of members possible. If your membership is missing a demographic, you are missing an opportunity to thrive.

How can you improve representation in your community? It can be helpful to break the process down into four steps:

1. Notice who is missing.

2. Analyze *why* the gap is occurring.

3. Identify and implement action steps.

4. Check in to see if the action steps are working.

Let's take a look at some ideas for how to approach each of these steps.

1. Notice who is missing.

❑ **Collect demographic data.** Yes, it can feel uncomfortable and invasive to ask your members to provide this personal data. But if your community wants to be more repre-sentative, this is the best way to do it. Most people are used to providing demographic information in lots of different contexts, so don't be afraid to ask. Before collecting the data, be sure to explain why you are collecting it and share exactly how the data will be used.

When collecting data, focus on the most important questions that are relevant to your community, and aim to be as open-ended as possible. Look at existing survey examples in your field and best practices for asking people about their demographics.

❑ **Address one excluded group of people at a time.** Be wary of falling into the trap of "what-aboutism" that people may use to distract others from equity goals. It looks like this: "Why are we making such a fuss about including more vegetarians? What about fruitarians?" Stay focused. The demographic data that you are collecting gives you a benchmark, so you'll be in a good place to start trying out ideas that might lead to real change in your community. It may turn out that by trying to close one gap the solutions you come up with will work for closing other gaps too.

2. Analyze *why* the gap is occurring.

❑ **Get to the root cause.** People often like to jump to the solution before really understanding the problem. Root cause analysis can help your community better understand what specific problem to address.

❑ **Ask for feedback.** The "5 Whys" may help your group figure out the issue, but it may only be able to get you so far. A more direct way to get

→ The "5 Whys"[16] is one common approach used to identify root causes. The basic idea is that you pose an issue, and then invite ongoing reflection into why that issue might be happening by con-tinuously asking, "why?" at least 5 times. By the end of this exercise, you may have come up with more than one conclusion. Test these conclusions (and assumptions) by collecting more data from the com-munity, and discussing these ideas with different people in the community.

→ Problem: We have no vegetarians in our community.

→ Why? Because all of our events are meat-heavy BBQs.
Why? Because the person who leads our events has always done it that way.
Why? Because it's easy.
Why? Because they've done it so many times before.
Why? Because we don't have any other volunteers who have offered to help.

→ Aha! The root of the problem. We need more event volunteers.

at the root cause is to ask people in the demographics you are missing about reasons for their lack of involvement. This may include doing a focus group or having individual conversations with marginalized members of the community. What barriers are in the way? What would make participation easier and more likely? We encourage you to listen to them with an open heart and mind, as sometimes the responses may make you feel defensive.

❑ **Examine your governance structure and public representation.** Have the same four people

---

[16] This process was originally developed by the Toyota car factory system. For more details about how this process works see: OD Serrat (2009). *The Five Whys Technique*. Asian Development Bank. https://www.adb.org/publications/five-whys-technique.

been making all of the major decisions in the community for the past several years? Are they all from a similar demographic? Your leadership may unintentionally be sending a message that makes some groups feel like they don't belong. Take time to look at your current representation to see if this could be contributing to the gap.

3. Identify and implement action steps.

❑ **Recruit an action committee.** Strategically recruit a team to work together to address the issue. Equity can be a charged topic, and having a thoughtful group of champions onboard will make it more likely that your cause will make some headway. Be mindful of elevating and centering the voices of those who fall within the gap population into the team, without asking them to do all of the work. The broader a coalition you can build to support the cause, the more likely it is to succeed.

❑ **Focus on solutions that address the root cause.** For example, prohibiting anyone over the age of 40 from joining your community is not necessarily going to encourage more people under 40 to join. Instead, if you determine that the root cause of why women under 40 aren't joining your community is because of their child care responsibilities, then your solution should be to remove that barrier. For example, you could have meetings at playgrounds or host virtual meetings with minimal expectations for participation ("turning on your video is not expected").

❑ **Pay attention to new members.** Once you've got a new member or two from the group you were focused on, chances are that, like any new members, they might not feel completely at-ease, especially if they are "the only one." Create a plan to provide excellent support for them along their membership journey. For example, you could introduce them to 2-3 members in the community who have things in common with them, so they get a head start on building their own connections within the community.

4. Check in to see if the action steps are working.

❑ **Recheck your data.** Repeating the same demographic survey a year later and then comparing the results is one of the clearest ways to see if you've made any progress.

❑ **Be aware that it's often more than one solution that might work in tandem.** It can be hard to pinpoint what, exactly, is having the greatest impact. Repeat your focus groups or include open-ended questions in your surveys that allow respondents to share what specifically helped them.

❑ **Keep going.** Once you feel like change is happening, you can move on to addressing the next excluded group of people (those fruitarians!). If you're lucky, maybe your current changes are already making your community less exclusive in more ways than one. Be aware that equitable communities are always shifting; you have to systematically and consistently work hard to keep full representation.

Pinpointing who is missing in your community, and addressing this issue, may require your community to have some deep conversations, and to also question your values as a community. You may be surprised, and possibly disappointed, in how others in the community react to your attempts to address the gaps. Many people haven't had much practice in talking about community access and equity, and your efforts will likely raise a lot of questions. What's important is that you remain focused on the goal of cultivating all potential community members, not just those who feel comfortable already in your group, or those who find it easy to show up.

As you made your way through this chapter, did it occur to you that there are gaps in your membership? If so, what are some first steps you could take to address the gaps?

NOTES

CHAPTER 5
Uplift Community Volunteers and Champions

A staff member once told me how difficult it was to keep volunteers on track. She described a challenging and frustrating circumstance where a member had volunteered to write a key report for the organization. It had been weeks, and the deadline was fast approaching. Yet, the volunteer had made no progress on the report, and the organization was counting on it. —Arika

People sometimes join a community simply to be a part of it, but others may join because they want to make an impact by getting actively involved. For Community Stewards, these are the moments we are striving for: when a volunteer offers to help. When this happens, we encourage you to do everything you can to assist a volunteer in finding a role that will be both helpful to the community, and feel uplifting to the volunteer.

You may also feel a little worried, because, as Arika's story illustrates, managing your volunteer power takes effort. When volunteers are not well supported, it can be damaging for everyone involved as conflicts arise. So here's your chance to think about how you can best support the success of your volunteers.

To start, we encourage you to find out what motivates them. Some common reasons that people may offer to volunteer include:

→ **They expect to personally gain from the role**. Some people may want job experience (e.g., video editor), to add a specific title on their resume that helps advance their career (e.g., Board member), or to demonstrate their leadership capability, such as by leading a working group or community of practice.

They might also like to network and get to know other people who they could lean on professionally in the future.

→ **They believe in the mission of the community**. These volunteers want to feel like they are pushing forward an agenda they believe in and that they are creating change and impact in the world. They may also feel that the community is doing a lot for them, and they want to give back.

→ **They find it enriching.** People often volunteer for things because they find it emotionally and personally enriching and fun. They enjoy the people they are working with, and want to deepen those relationships.

It is also helpful to know which type of work a volunteer has time, energy, and feels qualified for. Do they want to help out with a one-off event, hold a more time-intensive Board role, or take on a small recurring administrative task, like monitoring your social media pages?

Once you have an understanding of the types of volunteer roles a person may be interested in, you can increase your chances that things will go smoothly by following these tips:

- **Give volunteers a title and role description.** To make it easier for volunteers to step into a role in the community, a clear "job" description and title can be very helpful. Such clarity allows people to feel more ownership of their roles, and helps everyone in the community understand who is doing what. Some example titles are: Social media poster, Blog editor, Welcome team lead, and Calendar wizard. Making the titles fun, or allowing people to come up with their own titles can also feel motivating. Bullet out the details of the role, and be as clear as possible with what the responsibilities are and how much time it might take them to do the role successfully.

- **Be clear on your expectations.** The best types of volunteer roles are those that have very loose commitments and deadlines. That said, be very clear about your expectations around deadlines and parameters. Don't assume a volunteer sees the role or tasks with the same weight of importance as you do, and accept if things don't turn out exactly as you expected.

- **Separate paid roles from volunteer roles.** These two groups are very distinct, because they are motivated and incentivized to contribute to the community differently. If you are thinking about how to divide up responsibilities between staff and volunteers, it's actually quite simple: Staff do the things that no one wants to volunteer for. These are typically things that require sustained commitment, responsibility, accountability, and time—like bookkeeping, accounting, executive directing, grant administration, and general management.

- **Clarify legal obligations.** Volunteers should not be expected to wade into a legal or financial mess, or an ethical or political conflict that will take much more from them than simply time and motivation. Board members are an exception to this, and are often called into very dramatic and difficult decision-making positions[17]. If you are giving a volunteer a role that could have legal ramifications, make sure you let them know up front what their obligations are.

- **Be mindful of making someone "indispensable."** Volunteers should be able to step back from their role at any time without causing major disruption to the community. If one individual is holding too much responsibility, consider breaking up their role into smaller roles or providing them with a partner or two.

- **Give them space.** Another way to diminish someone's enthusiasm is to micro-manage them. Put your goals, action items, and plan together with your volunteers, and then give them the time and space to get their job done. Never "task" a volunteer with something, instead make suggestions and let them speak up if they want to do it.

- **Check in periodically.** Find out if volunteers are enjoying their roles and what support they need in order to get things done. People may not proactively come to you if there are problems, so reaching out and offering a listening ear is important. Remove barriers rather than construct additional hurdles. Volunteers are often dependent on people in leadership positions to give them the green light, provide materials/funding, or otherwise make their jobs possible, so once they tell you what they need—give it to them.

- **Help them pass the baton.** Create opportunities for volunteers to mentor and coach the next generation of volunteers. As new volunteers show up in your community, partner them up with a more veteran volunteer to learn the ropes and get support. You might even find that you can work yourself out of the job of onboarding volunteers by letting experienced volunteers take over.

---

[17] Board insurance, or Directors and Officers (D&O) liability insurance, is recommended to help legally protect volunteers that hold formal roles in an organization.

❑ **Recognize** "**Community Champions**." These are members who go the extra mile to consistently step up to help as volunteers, offer wise advice, and inject energy and life into the community. Community Champions are some of the best collaborators and volunteers you can hope to have as a Community Steward.

Community Champions may take on a role akin to that of a member of the Board of Directors or Advisory Board. They may also stay in the background by advising the community when they are called upon, promoting the community when they can, and keeping the community at the top of their mind while seeking out new opportunities that can benefit the community. They can also exist outside of the community itself. For example, they could be a funder who loves what the community is doing and wants to support it, or a leader of an adjacent community who is always interested in partnering on co-sponsored events and projects.

As you are thinking about supporting volunteers, keep an eye out for your champions, and bring them in when you need an extra boost of support.

Above all, value your volunteers. Value them for their time and willingness to share and contribute. Every little bit helps. If each person in the community could offer just one small piece, just think of what your community can accomplish.

In reading this chapter, what issues resonated for you related to managing your volunteers? Could you recognize someone in your community that you might call a Community Champion? Has reading this shifted your perspective on volunteering within your community, and, if so, how?

NOTES

CHAPTER 6
Be Mindful about Fees

A friend of mine had been volunteering in a new community for a few years. She told me that she loved the energy of the other volunteers and the community's social impact mission, and often encouraged others to join. The founders had minimal resources and time to run the community on their own, so they welcomed other members to step in—and they certainly did. Members started up social media platforms and made regular posts, helped to coordinate and host new programs, events, and speakers, and donated their skills like developing branding and a new membership management platform.

After a few years of this volunteer effort, the community really started to thrive. Members were finding real connections with each other, and also new opportunities. The membership number grew. It wasn't long before the founders stepped back in and implemented a membership fee. Suddenly, all of the community-developed resources were no longer available unless the members paid a high annual fee. For my friend, as a graduate student with a tight budget, the membership fee was outside of what she could afford. She felt that she had put a lot of time, effort, and heart into helping to build the community, but was pushed out as soon as the community turned into something that had monetary value. —Arika

There may come a point in your community's existence when a decision is made to charge dues or membership fees, or to raise the current rates. This can be a great way for your community to sustain itself, but charging dues also comes at a price: What if members don't have the financial ability to pay those dues? What if having to pay dues causes potential members to decide it's not worth it to them? What if charging dues causes social inequities within your community? How might volunteers feel about having donated labor to a community-owned resource that they must now pay to access?

As you look at fee structures, it can be helpful to start by grounding yourself in the core values and history of your community. Take a minute to reflect on the following areas:

❑ **Your culture.** Values like social equity, open access, and community-based can be the antithesis to "paying-to-play." If you value access, then your fee structure needs to reflect this.

❑ **Your cost.** What is the real cost to keep members on for free? For example, if it's a free Google group that requires the same amount of time to manage 20 people as it does to manage 100 people, then making sure that all 100 people pay a membership fee may not be necessary. However, if the community incurs a cost for each member, for example, a community that rents and shares a limited community garden space, then it might not make sense for your community to have free membership. Do the math and plan accordingly.

❑ **The value you offer in the community.** Does your community offer enough value? Is it unique and valuable enough that people will pay for it and feel happy with what they are getting in return?

❑ **Your origins.** Did your community begin with the message that you are community-based, and volunteers stepped in to get it off the ground? It can look like a bait-and-switch if community members aren't well integrated into the process of moving towards a membership fee model.

❑ **Your audience**. Is there a large income gap among your potential community members? Is your community intended to be international? If so, consider the World Bank country classification for income levels[18] when calculating fees.

❑ **Your messaging**. Paying dues can also feel empowering for community members, so don't shy away from considering dues or fees because you're worried about causing offense. If people value the community and feel a co-ownership of it, you may find that paying dues strengthens people's feelings of commitment.

Now that you've taken time to reflect on your values and history, take a look at these alternatives to a flat-feed due structure to see which ones might help you stay in alignment with how you show up in the world.

❑ **Minimal membership fees** can help members stay accountable, as well as supplement the costs of a community that might be mostly volunteer run. Work with your membership to figure out what would feel like a "minimal" fee. For some groups $20 a year might feel like a lot, while for some groups $1,000 might feel like a little.

❑ **Tiered membership** means you establish different levels of access to the community at different prices. The risk here is that it can unintentionally create a hierarchical structure in the community, such as by treating people who pay more as more valuable than other members. However, the benefit of a tiered membership is that members can have a more tailored experience.

What might you include in your tiers?

> → A free tier could include basic access to community resources like your website, videos or articles, and a public online social networking group.
> → A low-level tier could be a members-only area of the website that includes access to additional videos or articles and a message board, invitations to monthly meetups, and discounts to events.
> → Higher priced tiers usually include things that are more costly to provide, like access to services that require more time or skill by organizers, and free access to otherwise paid events.

A very important note here: Tiered membership is about allowing varying levels of access based on what members need, and not on what they can afford. In addition, a free tier helps people get to know the community, and either join at a higher level later or at least share about their experience with other potential members.

If you decide to go with a tiered membership option, you are encouraged to think about what to do if someone would like to access a higher tier, but cannot afford it. Do you offer scholarships? Do you fundraise to supplement those scholarships? What kind of system do you set up to be transparent in how you make decisions about these scholarships?

---

[18] World Bank (2023) "The World by Income and Region". datatopics.worldbank.org/world-development-indicators/the-world-by-income-and-region.html

❏ **Equity-based membership fees** allow your community to charge different amounts to different groups, for example, students and seniors, educators, historically marginalized groups (e.g. people with disabilities), nonprofit groups, or those who are currently facing hardships like unemployment or food insecurity may be given the option to pay less. On the other hand, those who are earning a solid income and are from historically-dominant groups (property-owners, fully-employed people, people working for large businesses), are encouraged to pay more.

In this model, fee levels can be self-selected by the members (honor system), or you can ask people to submit proof as to why they qualify for the rate they are opting into. To help people self-select, be sure to include a detailed description of what qualifies a member to receive each rate.

A risk in this model is that if everyone chooses the lowest rate, the community may be unable to cover its expenses. You may want to consider calculating your top rate so that it makes up the difference for what the lowest rate will bring in. We also suggest that you describe how your fee structure has been calculated, while reminding members that honoring the fee structure translates into being able to run the community effectively.

❏ **Pay-what-you-can** allows members to choose how much they want to contribute. It is helpful in this model to provide examples of what is a reasonable range, and to be clear about what your costs are, so people understand how far their fee will go. When providing a range, consider that most people will pick something in the middle. Unlike in the equity-based model, there are no set guidelines for who should pay what, rather, the scale is based on how much people feel the membership is worth to them.

Giving people a choice in how much to contribute towards a community membership allows people to feel that they have control over their assets and the value they place on the community. It opens up the possibility for big contributions, but also runs the risk of lower-than-hoped-for contributions. Set the bar high, and you may be pleasantly surprised.

If charging membership fees is new to your community or if you are planning big changes to your membership fee structure, we want to emphasize that it is wise to bring the options to your community to weigh in on.

How do people feel about the various models, and what are the advantages and risks of each one? Suddenly charging a lot for something that used to be free, or adding tiers where there used to be just one level can cause upset and confusion. Remember, your goal as a steward is to empower people to make the community better. Bringing them into these types of big impactful decisions is a great way to do that.

NOTES

SECTION II
GET TOGETHER

Reflect on this: What brings a community to life is when people connect, share ideas, and collaborate with each other.

When people think of "community," they usually think of a group of people getting together and doing something meaningful–whether it's enjoying a picnic, hosting a fundraiser, or making decisions in a meeting. And it's true, the heart of a community is often found through the events it holds.

Getting together as a community is what makes the community visible to itself. It helps members build relationships, get tasks done, and reach goals much more quickly than any long string of emails ever could.

But, as you may have noticed, getting people together in meaningful and intentional ways can take a lot of time and energy. Sadly, for reasons that we may find hard to pinpoint, our efforts sometimes fail to meet the goals we hoped to achieve.

In this section we offer ideas for how you, as a Community Steward, can help your community gather with more impact and ease. Our hope is to support you in thinking more deeply about how to be inclusive, and to design more powerful activities that build stronger connections, greater trust between members, and ultimately help you all get to where you want to be.

Events within a community can take all types of shapes and forms including those that support learning, social gatherings, fundraising events, networking-focused events, and plain-old meetings. No matter what type of gathering, there are a number of key points to keep in mind to help your get together feel both empowered and impactful:

❑ **Bring together a planning team.** Hosting a gathering always goes more smoothly when a team comes together to plan and facilitate the time. This is an excellent opportunity to build leadership skills within your community, and include more people in the process.

❑ **Decide on a budget**. Locations, food, materials… the costs of hosting an in-person gathering can really add up. Consider how you might raise funds to support the things you want to accomplish at the event to meet your goals. From asking for a registration fee, to doing an independent fundraiser, to soliciting donations, figure out with your community the best ways to remove financial barriers.

❑ **Be clear on your goals.** With any event, there is always the danger that you will try to do too much. The truth is, less is often more. Pick 1-3 big goals for the day, and make sure one of these goals focuses on participant well-being.

❑ **Find a location that meets your needs.** It's very important to choose a space that will best serve your purpose. For example, for a Board meeting, you may want a space that has lots of tables or walls, so groups can brainstorm activities on large sheets of poster paper. If you are hosting a wellness event, then a space with nature and sumptuous food might be key. When bringing together groups who don't typically interact, you may want to choose a space that is new to all parties to help people step outside of their usual way of being and thinking.[19]

❑ **Communicate. Communicate. Communicate.** Tightening up your communications with members before, during, and after your event can help increase the impact of your event and help members participate with more ease. Keep your communication short and to the point, being mindful of the fact that no one has time to read long missives.

We also want to point out that when groups gather together often, or have gathered in the same way for many years, events can start to feel "stale," causing people to feel on the fence about showing up. Choosing ways to get together that mix things up can help people feel more excited about both volunteering and attending. We hope that the following chapters will help inspire you to try out some new ideas, or refresh the get-togethers you already offer.

NOTES

---

[19] For some great tips on hosting impactful gatherings, take a look at Parker, P. (2020). *The Art of Gathering: How we meet and why it matters.* Penguin.

CHAPTER 7
Facilitate Mingling

> *I was invited to attend a virtual "happy hour" event for a new training cohort that I had just joined. It was set up for the cohort to get to know each other. Six people attended—about a quarter of the full group. The only person I knew there was the host who had invited me. All of the participants were men who were much younger than me and they clearly knew each other from previous activities, so I was already feeling like an outsider upon arrival. I turned my video on and smiled a Hello to everyone. Then, I proceeded to sit there for 15 min without anyone acknowledging my presence. The group laughed and chatted about things that I didn't have any context for and about people I didn't know. Finally, I turned my video off and exited without having said a word. It was so uncomfortable. —Arika*

Like bars, libraries, or public parks, many of the communities you are a part of represent "Third Places,"[20] meaning that they lie on a continuum between a person's home environment and their professional work environment. While you may smile and offer a quick hello to passersby, without a formal invitation or opportunity to connect, it's possible that you won't interact much further than this.

This is where introducing mingling activities in your community gatherings can help. Planned mingling can help make it less awkward for people to get to know each other better—whether it's at your annual potluck, silent auction, or strategic Board retreat. These activities help break up cliques and give people an opportunity to talk to someone who they don't often approach.

Below are some of our favorite activities, divided into categories based on their purpose. We encourage you to integrate your community or event theme into the questions prompts to give them more intentional meaning for your group. These mingling activities can also be converted to an online environment or vice versa.

☐ **Scavenger-hunts** are great for mixing the group up and giving people opportunities to meet lots of other people. Use these types of minglers when you really want to get a group active and talking to each other one-to-one.

→ **Are you the one who?** Without writing their name, ask each participant to write a fact or short story about themselves on a piece of paper (e.g., I once played trumpet at the start of a pro baseball game; I have seven sisters). They then hand you their paper, until you have collected them all. Now hand each person a random paper from the pile and let

---

[20] R Oldenburg (1989) *The Great Good Place: Cafes, Coffee Shops, Bookstores, Bars, Hair Salons, and Other Hangouts at the Heart of a Community.* Da Capo Press.

them try to find the person who wrote on the paper.

→ **People Bingo.** Prepare bingo grids that are 5 x 5 squares and put a fact or talent that someone might have into each square (e.g., I can speak three languages; I have visited the Grand Canyon). Pass out copies of the grid to each participant and give them a set amount of time to try to find people within the group who can sign their initials into each square. Play until someone fills in a line or the whole board.

→ **Find someone who…** Has the same birth month as you. Has the same favorite restaurant as you. Watches the same TV show that you do. Call out the prompts, and see how many people are able to find a match!

❑ **Things in common** minglers help build group cohesion and help people get to know where they may be the same or different from others in the group.

→ **I love my neighbor who…** Set up a circle of chairs so there are enough places for everyone, minus one. One person stands in the middle of the circle and shares, "I love my neighbor who…" and then states a fact about themself (e.g., who was born in Florida; who has a twin sibling). Anyone else who meets the shared criteria (the "neighbor") gets up and runs across the circle to sit in an open chair that is being vacated by another person who has gotten up and is running across the circle. At the same time, the person in the center also runs to sit in an open chair. Whoever is left in the center is the next person to share, "I love my neighbor who…"

→ **Would you rather?** Create a list of "would you rather" questions (e.g., Would you rather work from home or the office? Would you rather travel around the world or live in a nice house?). Choose sides of the room to represent each option and ask participants to move to the side that aligns with their response. Now ask individuals from each "side" to share why they picked that side. If they make a convincing argument, other participants may choose to switch sides.

→ **Pair/trio competition.** Divide participants into pairs or trios and give them a set amount of time to create a list of all of the things they have in common that cannot be seen by looking at someone (e.g., you can't say "we are both wearing sneakers" or "we both have brown eyes"). When the time is up, invite the pairs/trios to share their lists with the whole group. Who found the most things in common? Are there any things that everyone has in common? If you are doing this online, send the small groups into breakout rooms to create their lists before returning to the main room to share out.

❑ **Getting to-know you** minglers are great for when you already know each other on some level, but want to have fun and get to know each other better.

→ **Two truths and a lie.** In this classic game, each participant shares two things that are true about themselves and one thing that isn't true. This game is really fun if you make it related to the theme of your community. The rest of the group has to guess which fact is a lie. Continue until everyone in the group has had an opportunity to share their truths and lie.

→ **Which one of us has…** Pair up participants and ask them to each come up with a fact about themself (e.g., I can scuba dive; I am allergic to cats). Invite the pair to share the two facts with the group and let the group decide which fact is true about which person. If you are doing this online, pair people in breakout rooms first to come up with their facts, then play the game together in the main room.

→ **Show off a talent.** Invite each person to think of a quick talent they can show off (e.g., wiggling their ears; whistling the alphabet song; turning a cartwheel). Now have participants take turns showing off that talent!

❑ **Deeper-thinking minglers** are useful when you want to get your group warmed up to thinking strategically or working together to problem solve.

→ **What office supply are you and why?** Go around the room and invite each person to share which office supply (or household appliance or tool related to your community) they are, and why. This can also be done in small groups if people are sitting at tables.

→ **These are better than those.** Create a list of items related to the theme of your community, for example, a cooking club might use a list of kitchen tools and a book club might use a list of books. Let teams work together to decide on a hierarchy of the items based on any dimension they want. Does the garlic press belong higher on the list than the lemon juicer? Let teammates give their opinions and try to come to a consensus on what the order should be, then share their prioritized list and reasoning with the other teams.

→ **Random pairings.** In this activity, people walk around while music plays. When the music stops, they quickly pair up with someone nearby. Give a question prompt for the pair to discuss that relates to your theme. You could ask, "Why did you decide to come to tonight's meeting?" or "What do you appreciate most about our organization?" After a short discussion (3-5 minutes), start the music up again, and let people pair up with someone new and offer a new question prompt. Repeat 3-4 times to give people a chance to each meet and chat with a handful of group members. If you are doing this online, send people into breakout rooms for 3 minutes in trios to hold these discussions.

❑ **Asynchronous minglers** are activities that are organized for the whole group, but individuals within the group interact on their own time and not necessarily when the rest of the group is together.

→ **Partner meetups.** Create a list of random pairings of members, such as on a spreadsheet. Invite those partners to exchange phone numbers and provide a list of questions or prompts for them to discuss. Give the pairs a timeframe for the call (e.g., before our group meets again next month). At your next meeting, set aside time for partners to share back out with the whole group what they learned from meeting.

→ **Introductions.** Each person can share a brief introduction about themselves in a virtual space, such as on a specific thread or channel of an online Collaborative Workspace. People can post videos or written responses to a series of prompts like, "Name, where you work, why you joined this community, something you are learning/reading right now," etc.

→ **Photos shares.** Using a shared online space, like a Collaborative Workspace or Social Media, use a prompt to invite people to post photos related to your community. Then other people in the community can make guesses about what the photos are. For example, for your outdoor club, "Post a photo of your favorite trail, and let us see if we can guess where it is." Photos of pets, foods, nature observations, and locations all make good mingling conversation starters.

As you probably have noticed, most of these activity ideas can be done with endless modifications. We encourage you to use this list as a starting point. What questions might you include that would be illuminating and interesting for people? Which ones would help members feel like they are both having fun while connecting with others?

NOTES

CHAPTER 8
Organize Around a Common Issue

For years, I led a small collaborative group made up of scientists and practitioners around the topic of place-based community resilience. For a few months, we wondered why we were together and what our purpose was. Then, we settled on a writing project that focused on answering a single research question. We spent several years writing that peer reviewed paper[21], meeting monthly and then weekly. It was a wonderful experience where we developed a strong camaraderie and rapport between us. We learned each other's strengths and gaps, and knew who to lean on for expertise in data science or social science, or who had more experience working with federal government or non-profits. We felt that we were stronger and wiser together, and enthusiastically volunteered for tasks and helped support each other. —Arika

When people gather together to support and learn with each other by examining an issue of common interest, they build relationships, increase feelings of belonging, and create a shared community identity.

Perhaps most importantly, these smaller convenings help make things happen in your community. Intentionally bringing people together around specific topics, issues, or "problems of practice"[22] is a powerful way to inspire your community to work together.

What might organizing around a common issue look like in your community?

For some communities, as in Arika's example above, addressing a single topic or issue is the core objective that drives the entire group. For other communities, smaller problem-oriented groups are nested within the community, like a working group or a committee. These small groups foster a feeling of intimacy that helps people collaborate more easily with each other, as well as explore different interests or responsibilities within the community.

Before launching, or remodeling, a group that is focused on addressing a specific issue or topic, consider asking questions like in Table 8.1 to help determine the scope of the group, and to outline their structure and purpose.

---

[21] Virapongse, A., R Gupta, Z Robbins, J Blythe, R Duerr, and C Gregg (2022) How Can Earth Scientists Contribute to Community Resilience? Challenges and Recommendations. *Frontiers in Climate.* https://www.frontiersin.org/articles/10.3389/fclim.2022.761499/full
[22] State Support Network (2019) *Problems of Practice Toolkit: Action Planning for Rural Schools and Districts.* https://oese.ed.gov/files/2020/10/rural-problemsofpractice-toolkit-508.pdf

Table 8.1. A checklist of questions to help determine the scope of an issue-oriented group.

Question to ask the group	Description of the response to the question
What do we hope to accomplish?	Get clear on short and long-term goals for the group, and the resources and people needed to realistically do it.
How will we accomplish it?	Decide on the timeline, what activities are needed, and who is responsible for organizing and leading each activity.
How will we communicate and meet?	Determine how everyone will connect and communicate on a regular basis. Collectively set the frequency, duration, and location of your meetings.
How will new people join in?	Get clear on when new people can join the group, and how you might decide who can join.
How will we know if we have succeeded?	Determine how you will evaluate your success.
How will we share what we've learned?	Sharing updates helps the group feel successful, and helps people outside the group feel looped in. This could look like a regular update in a community newsletter, or a mini-presentation at a meeting.
What will we call ourselves?	Mirror/contrast the format of your name based on what other similar groups are called in your community. Be aware that if you don't come up with a name intentionally, it's likely that you'll end up with a name that you didn't necessarily choose.

Below is a list of some of the more popular types of groups that meet around an issue. See if you can identify times when you were part of these types of learning groups, or consider ways you might bring one or more of these groups into a community you are currently a part of.

❑ **Communities of Practice (CoP)**. These generally consist of people who share a common set of problems, interests, or concerns. For example, an online group of local gardeners who share what to do about the snail invasion, share photos of their blooms, and notify each other when the local nursery is having a sale. This group might also come together to tour each other's gardens and host an annual plant swap.

In the field of education, Professional Learning Communities (PLC) are a common type of CoP where teachers work together to improve their teaching skills and foster a collaborative learning environment. Another type of CoP are Consultation Groups. In these groups, colleagues share what they are currently struggling with. These communities often involve peer-coaching or listening circles, with opportunities for the group to help individuals problem-solve and think through how to overcome barriers they are facing.

❑ **Affinity Groups**. Power dynamics related to race, gender, age, language ability, and other factors cause imbalances of inclusion and feelings of safety that are needed for members to truly participate in a community. Setting up affinity groups for members who hold these marginalized identities can help them find and support each other as they navigate community spaces.

Employee Resource Groups (ERGs) are one type of affinity group. While often supported by an employer, participation is voluntary and led by the employees themselves. ERGs may host events, speakers, and lunches that are sometimes open to the greater community as opportunities to learn and celebrate the diverse workforce.

❑ **Working groups, Committees, or Teams**. These are small groups that work together to address a specific problem, project, or question that is valuable to the community and require more intensive attention. They often get together when there is enthusiasm to work actively on a project, and disband once they have accomplished their task or their momentum has waned.

❑ **Cohorts**. These types of learning groups typically involve an invitation/application and a set time period that they will be active. Members enter into a cohort at the same time, and have activities and opportunities to learn and share together. For example, your community might want to develop a cohort that is specifically for new members. Such a cohort can help new members build bonds with each other as they learn about the community and what it means to be a member.

Keep in mind, however, that when learning groups are embedded within larger communities, it is important to ensure that they don't feel like clubs within a club. Instead, learning groups are intended to be thriving places for small groups of people to connect and make progress on a problem.

To help avoid this issue, we encourage you to try these strategies:

→ **Increase transparency.** Develop a way for these groups to report back and share out their learnings periodically.

→ **Increase access.** Coach the groups to have different ways to be inclusive of the entire membership, so that they don't become shrouded in mystery or feel exclusionary.

→ **Support a structure**. Ensure these groups are following the same governance structures and accountability that are expected of the greater community.

It's pretty likely that at some point every community will find value in creating smaller sub-groups that get together to address a specific issue or topic. Remember that one of the most valuable assets of these smaller groups is that they can be fluid, by starting up when needed, and closing down when the learning or task is complete.

As you think about your community, what types of smaller groups already meet around specific issues? What other small groups might be of interest to members or helpful to your community at large?

NOTES

CHAPTER 9
Develop One-to-One Support Activities

Some years back, I had a wonderful peer mentoring experience that was organized by a community of small businesses that I was a part of. First, I filled out a Google form that asked me questions about my background, experience, and needs. Then the organizers matched me up with another person. The organizers provided helpful guidelines like: meet a minimum of once per month, engage in the mentorship activity for 3 months, and use an offered template to frame our meetings.

In our first meeting, my peer mentor and I easily decided on what expertise we wanted from the other person (I asked for a brand review of my business), since we had access to the information that the other person had provided on the form. We then came up with a plan for how we'd balance our mentorship trade, and what our vision of success was. We ended up meeting much more than once a month, and completed the program according to the organizers' guidelines. It was such a successful experience that we are now friends and continue to meet up on a regular basis to catch up. —Arika

Large get togethers are energizing, and smaller issue-focused groups are effective at making things happen. But there is nothing like formalizing one-to-one interactions between members to build the kinds of strong ties between individuals that underlie a vibrant community.

While it may seem a bit daunting to set up, one-to-one activities have a high likelihood of paying off. Here are some different types of one-to-one activities that your community might want to engage in:

❑ **Coaching.** Coaching involves one or more people providing support, reflection questions, and mostly a listening ear to another person. While coaching can be a skilled profession, there are some basic ways that anyone can help coach another person without having any expertise in the area that the "coachee" wants to grow in.

Peer coaching, where people take turns coaching each other, includes inviting members to pair up or organize into a small group. A protocol for the pairs/groups to follow looks something like this:

1. Invite each member of the coaching team to reflect on an area of growth or goal for themselves. For example, if your community is a tennis club, each member might pick an area of their playing that they want to improve on. Encourage teams to share their goals with each other, and to ask each other any clarifying questions.

2. Next, each member identifies any obstacles that might get in the way of reaching their goal. For example, maybe they don't have enough time to work on that area of tennis. Naming what might hinder progress and sharing it with the coaching team helps everyone understand what each person is struggling with.

3. Now it's time to create a plan of action. This area of coaching can be tricky. It is easy for our peers to want to offer advice and solutions, especially after everyone has just shared their goals and barriers to reaching those goals ("Well, how about you try playing tennis early in the morning, before your family wakes up.").

   In this coaching model the plan of action must be developed by the individual themself. This means that each person should come up with their own solutions and ideas for how to reach their goal before sharing their thoughts with the group.

   As members are developing their plans, it can be helpful to break each goal down into a series of "mini achievements" and to attach a timeline to each stepping stone. Breaking big goals into smaller pieces can enable people to stick to their plan and feel successful along the way.

4. Once the plan of action is created, it is helpful for the pair/group to set up a regular check-in time for them to report on any successes, breakthroughs, challenges, or insights they have experienced. Peer coaching relationships can last a few weeks, or years. Again, this is something for the individuals to decide for themselves, although we suggest that the schedule is discussed periodically so everyone knows what to expect.

If you are planning to introduce peer coaching into your community, you may want to set up a process to launch the effort, for example by providing training on the process and goals of the coaching. You might also want to set up a way for participants to share their progress with other pairs/groups engaged in coaching, so they can learn from each other what's working best for them.

❑ **Mentoring.** In contrast to coaching, where no specific expertise is needed, mentoring relationships are typically set up between someone who has a lot of experience or knowledge about a topic, and someone who is new to that area. Within your community, mentoring relationships can be useful for onboarding new members and handing over specific roles, or even be a central part of what you offer to members.

Like Arika shared in her story at the beginning of this chapter, someone can be both a mentor and a mentee simultaneously. For example, an individual can be mentoring someone else in how to write and publish the community newsletter, while at the same time be receiving mentoring from another (or the same) community member on how to deliver online workshops. In fact, setting up mentoring relationships in this way can help keep a balance so certain people aren't always seen as the "experts," but are both teacher and learner at the same time.

❑ **Peer-Centering.** Peer centering means that we listen to understand (as opposed to listening to respond or react). As an activity, peer-centering means creating a space for individuals to simply be heard and seen, without any type of counsel or response. In the activity, pairs of community members give each other non-judgemental listening space. One person sets a timer for a set period of time and has the floor to talk about a current challenge they are working through while the other person just listens; then partners switch.

In one of my community groups, we have a practice of dedicating 10 -15 minutes of our monthly meetings to peer-centering. We have a series of guidelines that includes an invitation to listen to understand, and not to respond, counsel, or coach the speaker. Each pair or small group sets a timer, and then takes turns simply talking about any professional stumbling block that is on their mind. For us, this time is valued for creating connections. It allows people to "ramble" on about an issue without having to stress about coming to a conclusion or decision. Having uninterrupted time to talk with a deep listener is a gift. —Eva

❑ **Accountability Buddies.** These accountability relationships are great for when there are two (or more) people who are invested in similar—but not shared–goals. Together, they help each other get their individual goals across the finish line. To begin this relationship, each accountability partner makes their specific goals clear (e.g., I want to walk for 30 minutes three times per week), and then they both decide on how they want to check in with each other on a regular basis to help address barriers and cheer each other on. Accountability buddies often work best if the participants set up recurring meetings to check in on each other, but can also simply be a scheduled text exchange. In this way, the goals that they set out to accomplish together stay at the top of their priority lists.

Keep in mind that as you work to set up these types of activities it is important to have a way for members to share when something isn't going well (e.g., they were paired with someone who always cancels the session last-minute), so you can intervene if needed. Setting up a point-person or committee for these activities is a great way to make sure they are thriving.

As you read through the list of activities, which ones did you realize are already happening in some way within your community? Were there any new ones that feel like they might be a good fit for you?

NOTES

CHAPTER 10
Get Creative

During the 2020 pandemic, I noticed that people often arrived at our virtual meetings very stressed out. I began using a tool called "Plink!" that enabled small groups to simultaneously create musical beats together using a shared link. Before sending the groups into breakout rooms, I would ask them to note their current stress level on a scale from 1 - 10. I would then send small groups in "breakout rooms" in Zoom and give them 5 - 6 minutes to play Plink! When they returned to the main room, I asked them to note what their stress level was again. Invariably, it was considerably lower after having played with Plink! —Eva

Play is an important part of learning—especially within social environments.[23] It may seem counter-intuitive or like a waste of time, but pausing to do something creative or "outside the box" with your community can work wonders for breaking you out of habituated ways of thinking or acting. If you are noticing that your community is lacking energy, going in circles, or having trouble resolving issues, it may be time to try something different.

We've listed some ideas here that you can try out to help your community get creative, collaborative, and unstuck together.

❑ **Co-create mosaics/patchworks**. In this activity, each person is given a small tile, square of paper, or piece of fabric and is asked to decorate it along whatever theme you choose. For example, you may ask everyone to write or draw something that is important to them about the community. The pieces are then assembled together and hung somewhere where everyone can see it.

❑ **Contribute to the completion of a puzzle or picture**. This could be a table set up with a puzzle, for people to pause at and work on any time they walk by and need a little break. It could also be a giant coloring page or outline (there are many types of these available online) that is hung on the wall or laid out on a table in a hallway, and a pile of colored pencils or markers for people to use to color in the image.

❑ **Generate music together**. Plink! is really fun, but you can also make beats in-person just on the table, or, better yet, by bringing in some pots and pans or other things that can be used to make noise. Humming, singing, and drumming are all alternatives, whatever seems like it might be fun and easy for your community to get into.[24] Karaoke can also be a really hilarious and engaging activity to do together.

---

[23] P Gray (2013) *Free to learn: Why unleashing the instinct to play will make our children happier, more self-reliant, and better students for life*. Basic Books.

[24] For more about these types of practices and ways to introduce the healing powers of making music together, we recommend Chapter 14, "Harmonizing with Other Bodies," from R Menakem (2017) *My Grandmother's Hands: Racialized Trauma and the Pathway to Mending Our Hearts and Bodies*. Central Recovery Press. p. 181-186.

❑ **Introduce a craft project.** It may have been years since members of your community glued popsicle sticks, strung beads, or cut out pieces of felt, but the fun of childhood crafts can do wonders for easing the mind, opening up conversations, and creating an environment of ease. Pick a project that is easy to do for everyone, and that is themed along the lines of your community or a barrier you are facing.

❑ **Make a mess.** Bring in fingerpaints, clay, or ingredients to make slime, and give your community a chance to get their hands dirty while painting, sculpting, or playing together. Want to make it even more challenging? Invite your community to use these materials to create something with their feet!

❑ **Build something together.** Lego actually has a whole system called "Lego Serious Play,"[25] designed for corporate teams to brainstorm and prototype solutions together, but any building material will do. Invite small teams to see how high they can build a card tower, or a structure with marshmallows and toothpicks, or with a random assortment of objects and a hot glue gun.

❑ **Repurpose.** How many ways can you come up with for repurposing a plastic bottle, old t-shirt, or paper towel tube? Giving your community an opportunity to think outside the box with something simple like a household object is a great way to warm up to thinking creatively about an issue your community is grappling with, and can be especially helpful in those too-long Board meetings.

❑ **Act it out.** Improv and role-playing can be really fun ways to examine issues from various perspectives. Theater of the Oppressed,[26] Play-back Theater,[27] and many other forms of improvisation invite people out of their habitual ways of being, and into someone else's shoes— or into an imagined reality—that can expand people's capacity for creative problem-solving.

❑ **Solve problems.** There's a reason "escape rooms" are so popular; it is really fun to work together to solve a series of problems or puzzles. You can actually purchase "escape rooms" in a box, but there are many other ways to introduce challenges, like riddles, collectively solving a Sudoku or crossword, or trivia related to the theme of your community.

❑ **Introduce new perspectives.** Reading, watching a movie, or listening to a speaker together can bring in an outside perspective and new ideas that inspire people to think differently. Using such "third objects" to stimulate discussion is especially powerful for exploring sensitive issues and helping people uncover otherwise hidden thoughts and feelings around related topics.[28]

While fun and relaxing in and of themselves, all of these activities can be made even more powerful when accompanied by carefully-crafted question prompts and follow up reflection questions. For example, if you've invited everyone to help complete a puzzle, you might post the prompt, "As you add a piece to this puzzle, think about what pieces you are adding to our community." Or invite people to write something on the back of the puzzle piece before they add it to the puzzle, and then later flip the puzzle over to read everything that was written.

We hope something on this list gets you feeling excited to introduce a creative activity into your next community get together. As you read through this list, which idea seemed like the best fit for your community? What might you try?

---

[25] Lego (n.d.) Serious Play. https://www.lego.com/en-us/themes/serious-play/about

[26] Boal, A (1974) *Theater of the Oppressed*. Ediciones de la Flor. and Boal, A (1992) *Games for Actors and Non-Actors*. Routledge.

[27] Developed by Salas, J and J Fox for more information at: https://www.playbackcentre.org

[28] Object-based Learning is a concept that has been around for a while, and especially within education. Here is one collection of academic work on the topic: Kador, T and H Chatterjee (Eds.). (2020). *Object-based learning and well-being: Exploring material connections*. Routledge. See also, https://eprints.whiterose.ac.uk/170539/1/1468794120972607.pdf

CHAPTER 11
Tell Stories

After the great 2004 tsunami that devastated towns and cities across the Indian Ocean, indigenous island groups like the Moken of the Andaman Islands and the people of Simeulue in Indonesia were expected to have suffered the same high casualties as more-developed places in the region. Surprisingly, it was found that within many of the local indigenous groups almost everyone had survived, while regions that held more recent immigrant populations had much higher deaths.

Why? Despite the fact that a tsunami had not been recorded in most parts of the region for hundreds of years, these communities had been passing down traditional stories of the early signs of a tsunami–domestic animals fleeing to higher ground, insects becoming silent, shallow waters suddenly retreating. People who had never experienced a tsunami before, saw the warning signs and ran for the hills. —Arika

A community is made up of people's stories. We all have reasons why we joined, why we stay, and why we want to be there. We might also have unhappy stories about why we left and what we experienced. Sometimes we don't know the meaning of our own story until we tell it. Listening to and learning from these stories is really what communities are all about.

As a Community Steward, you can provide opportunities to encourage members to share and hear each others' stories, so everyone can understand the community better. Some storytelling opportunities can be more formal, such as by sending out surveys or asking members to write blog posts. But often stories are unplanned, such as when someone might launch into a story in the middle of a meeting. While such moments may cause impatience among members, they can also be a chance to really listen to and appreciate people.

While stories may not provide quantitative data, they do provide detailed qualitative examples that can help to convince funders and prospective members about the success of your community. Stories can also help you and other leaders make decisions about the community that are based in empathy and understanding.

For example, someone might say "Online meetings make it really hard for people in the community to connect with each other. I don't think we should meet in this way." if you ask this same person to offer an example of what they mean, you might understand that they've had some bad experiences with poorly run meetings in the community, where they felt excluded and unheard.

To draw out stories from members and piece them together, we can turn to well-established fields, like ethnography (the study of the customs of different people and cultures) for inspiration. Ethnography is a field that has done a lot of work developing questions that encourage people to tell stories to build a more nuanced picture of a culture. Your community has a culture too, and hearing the stories of the people in your community can help everyone understand it better.

Some different types of story-telling prompts that are often used in ethnography[29] when talking to someone include:

---

[29] An older book, but still just as relevant today: Spradley, JP (1979) *The Ethnographic Interview*. Waveland Press.

→ Take a tour: "When was the last time you…" "Describe a time that…" "What was it like when you…".

→ Examples: "Can you give an example of what it was like…"

→ Experience: "What are some experiences that you've had with…"

→ Hypothetical: "If you were…" "What if…"

Here are some ideas for how to integrate story-telling into your community:

❏ **Include space for storytelling at the start or end of meetings.** Use your mingling activities and icebreakers to prompt short stories from people. For example, "Describe one of the best collaborative experiences you've had." Since these types of questions often take longer and require an element of trust, they generally work best in recurring meetings with the same small group of people, when people already know each other but want to know more.

An upside or downside of online get-togethers is that they tend to end abruptly. Once that hour is up, the meeting is closed and everyone is dismissed whether they are ready or not. There is little time for people to have the impromptu hallway or watercooler chats that they might have had if the gathering were in person. If you find that most of your gatherings occur this way, try to build in some extra time at the beginning or end of the session where people can just talk about whatever they want. At the end of a meeting, you could say: "I can stay on for a few more minutes if anyone wants to stick around and chat."

❏ **Collect stories but also honor them**. In this guide, we suggest more than a few times that surveys of your community are a great way to get feedback from them. When you do these surveys, include an open-ended question or two, like: "Why did you join our community?" or "What has your favorite experience in the community been so far?"

Importantly, when you get the results back, don't just treat it as data to analyze and tuck away for future reference. Read the responses and discuss them with your leadership team or with the community. While you might naturally be looking for patterns, also try to focus on the individual who is writing each story. What does the story tell you?

❏ **Discover stories together.** As a community, you are creating stories together. There are plenty of opportunities to help these stories emerge. Developing website content and other descriptions of the community for communication purposes is one great place for this storytelling to happen. Some communities also create resources like white papers, articles, and blogs to share about concepts and processes that they have developed, and story-telling is a natural part of this. What is the story of how your community started? How did your last event go? What are some successes from the community that could be shared?

❏ **Highlight individual stories through your community media**. If you've got a website, newsletter, or blog, you've already got a great medium for being able to share a member's story. You can ask members to share about what they do, who they are, and what they've been thinking about lately. On a website, you might consider shaping "testimonials" around a story of a member's experience. Remember to keep equity and inclusion in mind by being aware of who in the community has shared already, who is most likely to share again, and who you have not heard from yet.

As you get more embedded in your role as a Community Steward, it can be easy to become so high-level that all you see is the community and not the individuals who make it what it is. Introducing stories and storytelling into your communities can help remind you—and everyone else—that, above all, your community is made up of individuals, and there is so much to be learned in the tales you all tell. Where can you look for stories in your community? What might you learn?

CHAPTER 12
Fundraise

In 2009, a frustrated group of friends in Helsinki were watching another international climate change summit fail. They wondered what they could do themselves to change the economy. After much planning, they developed a neighborhood "credit exchange" in which participants agreed to exchange services with each other, from language translations and swimming lessons to gardening and editing. The Helsinki Timebank, as it was later called, grew into a robust parallel economy of more than 3,000 members. With exchanges of tens of thousands of hours of services, it has become a socially convivial alternative to the market economy, and part of a large international network of timebanks. —Arika

While it's often thought of as just a means for increasing revenue, fundraising can actually be broken down into two objectives: the "Fund" (money), and the "Raising," which includes fostering meaningful interactions between members, spreading the word about the work of the community, and relationship-building all around.

Below we outline some common fundraising models used within communities. As you go through the list, think about how well each one fits with the mission and values of your community, so you don't raise funds in ways that feel exploitative or off-mission.

Which model you choose might also depend on how much organizing energy and accounting resources you have the capacity for. Any kind of organized event takes quite a lot of preparation, implementation, and coordination across different people. On the other hand, governmental grants often require that you keep a tight record of all expenditures, complete yearly audits, and submit timely reports to funders. We encourage you to choose a fundraising method that won't over-burden you in ways that you are not set up to handle.

Take a look and see which of these models align best with you and your community:

❑ **Dues/Membership Fees**. This is probably the most commonly used funding model for communities, since it's relatively straightforward. Dues are charged to each member at a set time, usually annually or monthly. Memberships can be offered to individuals or to organizations. Online platforms can help you manage timely payments, such as by setting up an auto-pay system.

❑ **Board of Directors**. If your community has nonprofit status, it is customary for members of the Board of Directors to contribute donations to the community or to fundraise within their contact network. This model could violate your equity and inclusion principles, however, especially if you have (or want to have) Board members who are early in their careers or otherwise do not have readily available funds. Some things to keep in mind when using this model:

→ Was fundraising discussed as part of the job description for your Board? If not, how might you describe fundraising in a way that is equitable to all Board members?

→ What ideas does your Board have in helping to raise funds?

❑ **Tokens or Timebank.** While fundraising is usually associated with money, you may also want to consider the value of donated time, which is also known as "in-kind support" or "pro bono" contributions. Like in Arika's story, with a tokens or timebank model you exchange something besides money, like time, skills, and expertise.

❑ **Organized Events.** Think of this as charging an entrance fee. For example, maybe you organize a concert, gala, or trivia night with paid admission, host a haunted house and collect money at the door, or organize an online seminar or workshop and sell tickets via an online platform. Money can be raised via ticket sales, raffles, or auctions (more on those below), and fun can be raised by the delicious food and drink, team competition, or watching each other on stage.

While events have the potential to be fun and successful, they can often be the most work-intensive. Good marketing is also essential. It can be unclear how much money you will raise through your efforts, however, as attendance can fluctuate, and the costs of putting on an event may eat into a large percentage of your proceeds. Some questions to consider include:

→ What kind of event would be fun for guests? Consider surveying people about their interests and opinions on what would make the event feel inspiring and connective. Can you include a "fun-raising" goal? How will you know if you've met it?

→ Is there a team that would be willing to take on the logistics and coordination?

→ How will you advertise? How can you best predict attendance and profit?

→ Are there various price points or different types of tickets? Giving people a range of options can make events more accessible, including a free option if it makes sense.

❑ **Raffles and Auctions.** Collecting prizes from your community (and beyond) and then offering them back to your community (and beyond) is a tried and true way to raise funds while making everyone feel like they are getting something in return. Some localities also have laws about raffles, or games of chance, so look into what is allowed in your area before going with this option.

If you have the volunteer or staff power to make it happen, here are some decisions you will need to make:

→ What types of items will be most interesting to our community? Can you find a range of price points so that there's something for every budget?

→ Is delivery of items an issue?

→ Will you host this online or in person? Will this be part of another event?

❑ **Sales Events.** This can be a yard sale, craft sale, or the ever-beloved bake sale. You can charge community members to host a table (e.g., $100 for a table to sell crafts), ask for a percentage of sales, or have people donate their items and all of the funds go to the community. Some decisions to make include:

→ Who will provide the tables and chairs?

→ Where will the cashbox be? What types of payments will be accepted?

→ Are there any laws around sales taxes (e.g., vendor's licenses) that will need to be addressed?

❑ **Services.** What services could you offer to people both inside and outside of the community (e.g., dog-walking, garden consultation, editing documents) that are in line with what your community is working towards?

This model can be combined with the membership model, for example, some services might be offered free to all paying members (one dog-walking session a month), while additional services may be provided at a discounted cost for members (20% off for additional dog-walking sessions).

For this funding model to be both community-centered and provide a good cost-benefit balance, you'll need to consider:

→ What types of services would be rewarding for your community to put together and offer?

→ Are there services that members of your community are willing to donate so that your community can maximize profit?

→ Who will provide the service, and who will manage and oversee the sales?

❏ **Contests.** Paying $20 to enter a pie-baking or karaoke contest can be a fun way to raise money. The winner gets a percentage of the entry fees, while your community treasury takes the rest. Activities like carnival games or guessing games are also part of this category, and all of these are easily combined with any of the other events outlined in this chapter. Some decisions to make:

→ What kinds of contest activities would community members enjoy participating in?

→ What kinds of prizes would feel meaningful to community members?

→ How "competitive" is your contest? Could you incorporate funny prizes and not just award a first, second, or third place set of ribbons?

❏ **"A-Thons."** These generally involve each community member collecting small donations from a broad group of contributors for completing a task. In a bowl-a-thon, you might ask people to "sponsor" you for $1 per pin you knock down. In a walk-a-thon, the $1 could be per mile or minute walked. What's appealing about "a-thons" is that your whole community can participate at the same time, which builds relationships and can be really fun. Some decisions to make include:

→ What activity would make the most fun "a-thon" for your group?

→ What platform or method will members be asked to use to collect donations?

→ Will you offer prizes to people to collect the most funds, or to anyone who participates?

❏ **Sponsors.** This means partnering with a company or organization who becomes a formal sponsor by committing to give you funding or other support services. This model usually requires building strong relationships with a sponsor, as well as having a very strong value proposition that aligns with the mission of the sponsor. Be sure that the sponsors you choose align well with the mission of your organization. For example, if your community is centered around environmental conservation, you probably don't want to be sponsored by a business with a poor track record in environmental protection. Some things to consider:

→ Are members of your community connected to companies that might be interested in sponsoring your work?

→ What businesses are in alignment with what your community is trying to do?

→ How can you acknowledge and promote your sponsors, so that they feel that they are getting some advertising or support in return?

❏ **Donation Drives.** This approach is often used by humanitarian or social impact initiatives like the Humane Society or Red Cross. You might send out emails to a list of potential donors asking for monetary donations or donations of items (e.g., gardening tools, books, or spare bike parts) that you need for your community.

If your community or its fiscal sponsor has a tax deductible status as a nonprofit (known as a 501(c)3 in the U.S.), you may be able to provide a letter that acknowledges the gift as tax-deductible, which is sometimes an incentive to donors. Be sure to also check if there are any legal tax structures that require you to have a license in order to solicit donations. To use this model, some questions to ask yourselves:

→ Is this a short-term push for donations (e.g., a 24-hour match event), or ongoing, such as a "donation" button on your website?

→ Is there a particular fundraising goal that everyone is working towards, or is it open-ended?

→ How will you acknowledge, thank, and/or report back to donors?

❑ **Crowdfunding**. This approach involves using an online platform like Patreon (for recurring individual support) or Kickstarter (for broadly soliciting a proposal) to solicit funding by having a clear goal and benefit for patrons, such as delivering regular content or a product. The biggest challenge with this approach is that you will have to convince people that being a patron is worth their money, and deliver on your promises. Some things to consider:

→ Do you feel that you have a large enough base that if you ask for a recurring donation, it would bring in enough profit to be worth the effort?

→ Are there various donation levels you could offer? What would the "perks" be for each level?

→ Does your community have enough recurring content or expertise to share with supporters? Who would manage collecting and sharing this out?

❑ **Grants**. Governmental and philanthropic funding sources are available to help support community building efforts. These usually require doing research by looking at funders' websites for "requests for proposals" (RFPs), or joining a website or mailing list that gathers these announcements together. When writing grants, being able to articulate the value that you are bringing forward, and making sure it balances out with how much funding you are seeking, is extremely important.

Grant writing and reporting can be time-consuming and require good writing skills, both of which might be burdensome to your community, especially if the grant isn't very large. Some communities hire professional grant writers to help with proposals. Some things to consider:

→ Do you or any of your members have grant-writing experience that could be lent to this process?

→ What type of grant might fit with the purpose of your community?

→ Is your community eligible to apply for the grant? If not, is there another organization you could partner with to submit the grant together?

Keep in mind that you really only need enough funding to keep yourselves going. If a simple once-a-year call for donations works for you, go with that! While it's exciting to have money on hand, there really is no prize for raising more funds than you need. As you read through this chapter, which option(s) seemed like something that might help your community reach both its "fund" and "raising" goals?

SECTION III
BE INTENTIONAL WITH POWER

Reflect on this: All organized bodies have a power dynamic, whether it's named or not.

Can you recollect a specific event or interaction within your community that surfaced an especially charged dynamic? Maybe it was…

- → At a planning session when a committee discovered that someone had made critical changes to an event without consulting others in the group.
- → A conversation where someone kept talking over someone else.
- → One person assigning tasks to someone else during a meeting without first asking permission.
- → A person taking credit for something that someone else did.

What you witnessed was a power dynamic in action.

The moment a power dynamic reveals itself is usually the expression of something that has been building up energy for weeks, months, or years before it eventually comes to a head or gets noticed. If nothing is done about it, it will likely become a norm within your community—making people feel uneasy or silently chasing people away, until there is no one left to energize the community.

Because of this, an important part of community stewardship is noticing and steering power dynamics so that they're used for the greater good of the community. It means being aware of your own power as a Community Steward and the pieces of power that are hiding in the corners of your community, waiting to surface.

Much of this guide is about managing power dynamics in one form or another. In this section, our goal is to help you become more aware of these dynamics, so that you can identify what is happening and have a better idea of where to look for solutions.

As you start your search, there are a number of places where power dynamics are most likely to surface. Take a look at the areas outlined in Table III.i, and note which ones have caused conflicts within your community.

Table III.i. The places in a community where power dynamics are likely to be present.

Power Dynamic Locations	How it Might Show Up
Decision-Making	Who gets to decide what? Who makes a final decision? Whose voices are considered before making decisions?
Membership	Who decides who can/can't be a member? How transparently are membership decisions being made? Who decides when someone is asked to leave the community?
Meetings	Do some people talk more than/over others? Do some people always show up, or never show up? Who is allowed to speak or get on the agenda, and how often?
Leadership	How welcoming and inclusive are people in leadership positions? How approachable and responsive are they? Who has access to leaders and feels heard by them?
Communication	Who is given access to share information or comments? Who decides what information gets shared? Who manages edits? Are certain people intentionally left out of conversations? Who decides that?
Events	Who shows up at events? Who feels like they belong, has fun, and wants to attend again? Who makes decisions about what, where, and when?
Fundraising	Who is setting prices? How are dues/fees/charges determined and collected? Who decides how much and where funds are spent?
Behavior Expectations	Does your code of conduct reflect that of a dominant culture? Do you require people to introduce themselves in a certain way? Do your rules work for the context of some people but not for others?

As you read through that list, did any of them feel like they could be problematic in your community?

In this section, we will invite you to peek into a number of different corners to see where you might address power imbalances. This includes thinking about how you show up as a leader, as well as reconsidering the language you use, your governance model, and your decision-making processes.

As with all of the suggestions we offer throughout this guide, we encourage you to be kind to yourself. Shifting power dynamics is not an overnight endeavor; it can take years, and there are often bumpy sections along the way. Pick one easy place to start, and go from there.

CHAPTER 13
Reconsider What Leadership Looks Like

My kids love reading Calvin and Hobbes. One of the themes that emerges periodically in the comic is the "club" that Calvin and Hobbes invented. They have songs, they have rules about who can join, they have costumes. And they constantly squabble over who is the boss. Even though it's mostly ridiculous, there is so much that is recognizable in the way that they construct and play out their leadership roles and power dynamic in their community of two. It is funny, but also true to how it often seems to happen in real communities! — Eva

While power dynamics can surface anywhere within a community, an important place to start is with yourself, since as Community Steward, you are often the de-facto "leader" of the community.

→ Do people often (always) turn to you to make decisions or answer questions?

→ Do you have a hand in most things that happen in the community?

→ If you stepped back, could the community run without you?

The interesting thing is, power in communities tends to shift over time, especially as a community gets older. On the next page we outline three stages of development that you might encounter as your community evolves, and how this might affect how much power the Community Steward holds in each one. Notice how at the top of the pyramid, power is more concentrated in that individual, while the farther down you go, the more dispersed it becomes, with the community being the base that can support the entire structure.

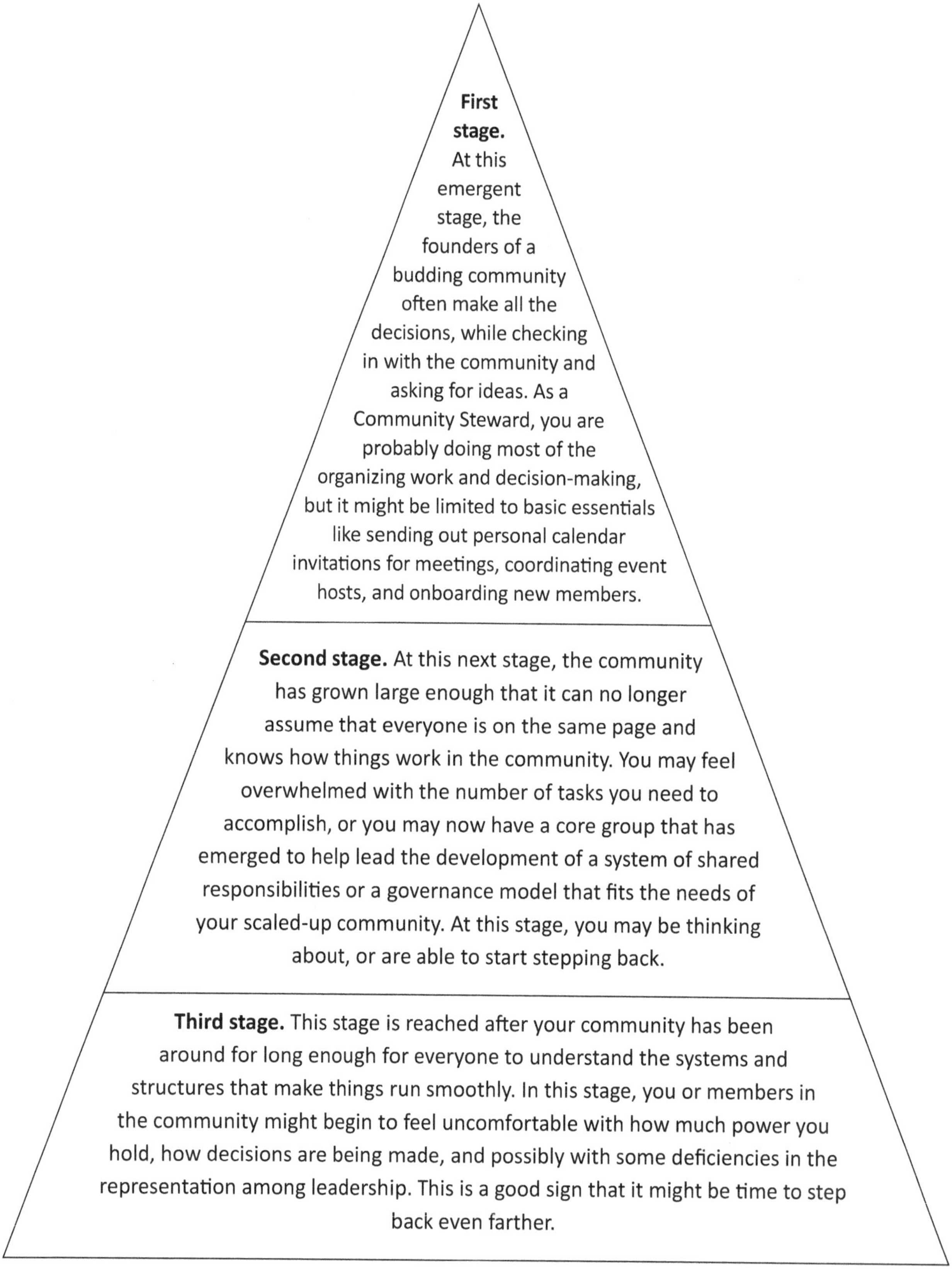

First stage. At this emergent stage, the founders of a budding community often make all the decisions, while checking in with the community and asking for ideas. As a Community Steward, you are probably doing most of the organizing work and decision-making, but it might be limited to basic essentials like sending out personal calendar invitations for meetings, coordinating event hosts, and onboarding new members.

Second stage. At this next stage, the community has grown large enough that it can no longer assume that everyone is on the same page and knows how things work in the community. You may feel overwhelmed with the number of tasks you need to accomplish, or you may now have a core group that has emerged to help lead the development of a system of shared responsibilities or a governance model that fits the needs of your scaled-up community. At this stage, you may be thinking about, or are able to start stepping back.

Third stage. This stage is reached after your community has been around for long enough for everyone to understand the systems and structures that make things run smoothly. In this stage, you or members in the community might begin to feel uncomfortable with how much power you hold, how decisions are being made, and possibly with some deficiencies in the representation among leadership. This is a good sign that it might be time to step back even farther.

Figure 13.1. Community power dynamic shifts over time.

Another way to look at your own power and role in the community, is to identify your current leadership style. Take a look at the table below and notice which style(s) you currently fall into. They are organized roughly by most tightly held power at the top, to more loosely held power towards the bottom. And please note, there is no right or wrong here, just notice!

Table 13.1. Leadership styles and an example of what the model looks or sounds like.

Leadership Style	What it looks/sounds like
Autocratic/Authoritarian Leader	I'll make the call on what needs to be done.
Bureaucratic Leader	We have some fixed rules, and I am here to make sure we follow them.
Transactional Leader	I will motivate you through rewards (or penalties) for going along with (or deviating from) the program.
Charismatic Leader	Let me help guide you.
Transformational Leader	I want to inspire you and give you the power to drive change on your own, and I will model the creativity and initiative I'd like you to take.
Coaching Leader	I see everyone's strengths and areas of growth, and will help you set goals and processes for your improvement.
Democratic Leader	I'll make decisions after everyone has had a chance to weigh in.
Collaborative Leader	I believe in bringing multiple "leaders" to the table to work together to drive change.
Authentic Leader	I take the back seat in a leadership setting by supporting and guiding other facilitators and leaders[30].

What we want to emphasize with these tables, is that when too much power is concentrated in yourself or a small group of individuals, not only does it disempower the broader membership, but it can also lead to burnout amongst those who are in leadership positions. If you are feeling this in the community you are stewarding, we offer these suggestions to help move power in your community further down the pyramid/table.

❑ **Expand your leadership style.** Try taking on different leadership styles to provide more balance of power in your community. For example, if you feel like your community is always looking to you as a "Charismatic Leader," it may be helpful to try being more of a "Democratic Leader" and asking your community to weigh in on important decisions. (But note, being a "Collaborative Leader" can be more than is needed in some situations–when those outdated reimbursement forms need to be reformatted, everyone would probably be relieved for an "Authoritative Leader" to step in and get it done!)

❑ **Delegate.** There are many reasons why you may hesitate to delegate. You may feel like explaining the task to someone else takes longer than just doing it yourself, or that they will not do it as well as you can, but it is a critical strategy when you are looking to transfer more power to members. Start with small, timebound tasks that won't have a major impact on your community

---

[30] This is also known as the concept of "leading from behind". See: Scharmer, CO (2009). *Theory U: Learning from the future as it emerges.* Berrett-Koehler Publishers.

if something goes wrong, and build up to larger, longer, more important tasks as time goes on.

❑ **Pause**. If someone comes to you with a question, instead of providing an answer right away, pause and ask the person what they feel the answer is, or should be. Making space for community members to fill in the blanks is a great way to step back so they can step up.

❑ **Invite company.** Encourage members to join you in whatever task you are doing. This not only makes it more fun, but helps them learn the ropes by working alongside you and builds feelings of shared ownership and "we're in this together."

Self-awareness is a huge part of being a Community Steward. We encourage you to return to this chapter periodically to check on how you're doing and where you're currently at in your power journey. Remember, holding power is not a bad thing, but it's important to know how to let some of it go for the good of your community. What suggestions in this chapter might make sense for you to lean into?

NOTES

CHAPTER 14
Develop Thoughtful Governance Structures

One weekend my family and I were meandering around our town on a lovely summer day. Soon we found ourselves asking the usual question: Where should we go for lunch? My daughter always says the same thing: a poke wrap. These days, I'll often lean towards spicy ramen or pho, but will tick off other choices too. My spouse and son are the wild cards. Most times, my spouse will go with whatever we all decide, and my son is often unpredictable as to whose idea he might back.

Is it a consensus? Sometimes. Is it authoritative? Often yes, especially when I can't bring myself to eat another poke wrap. Is it bottom-up? To some degree it always is (try making a kid eat something they don't want to). Most often we'll find an option that everyone can compromise on. Or, maybe we already ate poke wraps last weekend and my daughter understands that it's someone else's turn to choose. —Arika

Before you say "We don't have a governance structure in our community," be aware that if your community is operating, you do have a structure, whether or not you know what it is[31]. In addition to how decisions are made, community governance includes the overall framework of policy, processes, rules and norms, and assumptions around authority and responsibilities. Governance approaches are often guided by a community's shared needs and values.

Here are some examples of how different aspects of governance are demonstrated through community functions:

Policy:
- → Guidelines for approving budgets/financial decisions
- → Steering overall strategic direction and priorities

Processes:
- → Controlling membership onboarding/off-boarding
- → Setting up decision-making protocols

Rules and norms:
- → How and why a member reaches out to other people in the community

---

[31] Such informal governance structures are typical of "commons", which are shared resources managed by users for their own direct benefit. Governance of commons champions the idea that community empowerment is an effective and sustainable means for managing shared resources. See the seminal book by Elinor Ostrom that led to her Nobel Prize win in 2009: Ostrom, E (1990) *Governing The Commons: The Evolution of Institutions for Collective Action*. Cambridge University Press.

→ Knowing how to collaborate with and credit other community members

Assumed authority and responsibility:
→ Who determines and documents final decisions
→ Who takes responsibility for the outcomes of decisions

Since the late 1970's, approaches like participatory research, community-based management[32], citizen science, and open science have highlighted the importance of balancing out perspectives and power within communities. By allowing a broader range of people to be able to take part in governance, the results of community activities become less myopic and more impactful.

The best governed communities we've come across have established a balance between different kinds of governance approaches[33] depending on the circumstance. For example, in the U.S. we use a democratic model to elect government officials, but local officials may make decisions in ways that are autocratic.

Take a look at some examples of different governance models in Table 16.1. Note whether any of them describe your current model, or a model you may want to learn more about.

---

[32] Paolo Freire's seminal book that introduced the controversial idea that learners should be co-developers of knowledge is widely considered to be the ideological birthplace of participatory and community-based concepts, see Freire, P (1970). *Pedagogy of the Oppressed*. New York: Seabury Press.

[33] For examples of communities that balance top-down and bottom-up governance models, see Virapongse, A, J Gallagher, B Tikoff (2024) Insights on sustainability of Earth Science data infrastructure projects. *Data Science Journal* 23: 14, pp. 1–27. DOI: 10.5334/dsj-2024-014

[34] Sociocracy for all (2023) "Sociocracy vs Holacracy: what are the similarities and differences between them?". www.sociocracyforall.org/sociocracy-and-holacracy-a-comparison/

Table **16.1**. Different governance models, and key characteristics and notes about each model.

Governance Model	Key Characteristics	Notes
Autocratic	One person makes decisions and leads all key community functions.	Often present in newer communities or when an emergency situation arises.
Board-Led	A group of designated individuals lead community functions for the community.	Boards may solicit feedback from the greater community to incorporate into their decision-making process, and solicit the help of working groups to carry out tasks or gather information.
Sociocracy/ Holacracy[34]	The community is organized into clusters of individuals that lead and make decisions about portions of the community; a process of consent decision-making is used.	May be time-consuming, but the goal is that all members will feel heard and in agreement with the decisions and direction of the community. The "lift" of running the community is shared.
Democracy	Community members vote on decisions and elect leadership, who they entrust with running the community and making decisions on their behalf.	"Majority rules" can leave community members who didn't vote for the leadership team feeling unheard or disgruntled.
Do-ocracy[35]	Any individual who is willing to do the work takes on leadership and decision-making within the community.	People without the time/energy to take on work may disagree with decisions and feel unheard.
Peer Governance[36]	Based on the concept of "commons," where individual benefit is gained via the group, and rules are developed while bound by basic principles that serve to sustain the shared commons.	This approach is most appropriate when a community has distinct commons to manage together, such as physical or knowledge resources.
Cooperative[37]	The community is owned by members of the community, and each member has an equal say in how the community is run, and takes on a share of the labor.	Reaching agreement amongst a large group of people can be difficult, and managing the disbursement of tasks can be cumbersome. The community is often sustained through membership dues and contributions.

---

[35] A well-known example of do-ocracy is the Burning Man festival. Do-ocracy is sometimes associated with the term "direct democracy". A good description of how do-ocracy works in practice is included here: CommunityWiki (2021) "DoOcracy" https://communitywiki.org/wiki/DoOcracy.

[36] Bollier, D and S Helfrich (2019). Free, fair, and alive: *The insurgent power of the commons.* New Society Publishers. https://freefairandalive.org/

[37] International Cooperative Alliance (n.d.) "Cooperative identity, values & principles". https://ica.coop/en/cooperatives/cooperative-identity.

NOTES

CHAPTER 15
Decide How to Decide

I was involved with co-leading a community-centered organization that had hundreds of members. Initially, most of our decisions were made unilaterally by two co-leads. Over time as we got more organized, we began including committed community members into decision-making—mostly by having regular group meetings where people shared ideas and agreed on what should be done. When we began making more ethically difficult decisions that had high potential for bias (and harm) by decision-makers, we started using consent decision-making[38]. While we found consent decision-making to be really effective for us, it was also really time-consuming to do properly. It would have been too much work to use consent decision-making for every tiny decision. —Arika

Our days as humans are filled with a million tiny decisions. Some of those decisions are easy (it's raining today, I'll bring my umbrella), and some can cause extensive consternation (should I quit my job??).

The same is true within your community; throughout its lifetime, thousands of micro and macro decisions will be made. The question is, who, how, and when do these decisions happen? There is nothing that will disempower members more quickly than by having only top-down, opaque, and non-inclusive decision-making processes.

As Arika emphasized in her story, not all decisions can be made using the same process. In order to determine which process to use in which situation, you will need to consider factors such as:

→ Have you made a similar decision like this in the past that you can refer to?

→ Who does the decision impact? Does it impact all, some, or a few members of the community?

→ Is more information needed? Should other people be involved in this decision?

→ How urgently must the decision be made?

→ What are all the options for decision-making? What is the potential for harm and benefit that may be caused by each option?

Rethinking how decisions are made is the ultimate test of your openness to spreading out power. Please know, you do not need to suddenly throw all decisions out to the community. That would likely cause confusion and exhaustion, especially for a group that isn't accustomed to being involved in that way. However, to build an empowered community, you'll have to figure out ways to be as inclusive as possible with the people who are most impacted by decisions: your members.

---

[38] Consent decision-making was developed by sociocracy practitioners. Rau, T (2022) Consent decision making. [blog post] Published by Sociocracy For All. https://www.sociocracyforall.org/consent-decision-making/

Because members may be new to decision-making for the community, it may be helpful to start by involving them in the process of evaluating the options. Examples of how to do this are:

❑ **Plus-Delta T-Charts.** This strategy allows members to voice what they feel are the positive and negative aspects for each option being weighed. To use this method, a t-chart is created, with "plusses" (things that will work well) being listed on one side, and "deltas" (things that may not work as well) being listed on the other. This is a good way to make the attributes of each option transparent to all community members and solicit their input. You could also use the labels "pro" and "con" here, although that may set up a binary dynamic that is better avoided.

❑ **Rubrics.** A rubric is essentially a "scoring guide" or set of criteria that can be used to help you evaluate decision options. For example, a very common rubric for evaluating decisions looks like a box with four quadrants as in Table 17.1. Choices can be sorted based on these four criteria (or any other criteria you want to use). This is a good approach to use if you are trying to get more clarity on which options meet criteria you have set.

Table 17.1. A rubric for evaluating decisions based on required Effort (low/high) and expected Impact (low/high).

	Impact (high)	Impact (low)
Effort (high)	High Effort + High Impact	High Effort + Low Impact
Effort (low)	Low Effort + High Impact	Low Effort + Low Impact

Once options have been weighed, decisions need to be made. As you read through this list, notice which ones you already do, and which ones might be worth bringing into your community. We encourage you to do more research into how each of these different approaches are used, and reflect with other community members which options to try.

❑ **Approval Vote.** This is when the vote is either "yes" or "no." As in, "Do you approve of the new membership fees that have been developed by our finance committee?" For example, Robert's Rules of Order[39] usually calls for a vote to approve things like past meeting minutes, the current agenda, and budgets. While this approach relieves members of having to wade through all the options and details, make sure to include the backstory to any proposal so members have context around how the final options were chosen.

❑ **Consensus.** This is a decision-making process in which all parties come to an agreement on the decision (i.e., everyone says "yes" or "I can live with this"). This option is good for major decisions where you want everyone to be on board, but can take a lot of time if people are struggling to find middle ground.

❑ **Consent.** In contrast to consensus, consent decision-making aims to come to a decision that no one objects to. The decision-making process involves presenting a proposal to the group, then allowing the group to ask clarifying questions and proposing amendments until no one has objections to the final proposal.

❑ **Random selection.** Think of this as "flipping a coin." There are actually situations where you might want to use this, believe it or not. Heads, you go with the new logo; Tails, you stick with the old logo. The fun thing about using this

---

[39] Robert's Rules of Order are a set of parliamentary proceedings that many nonprofit organizations use as part of their governing structure. Read more at: Robert III, HM, DH Honemann, TJ Balch, DE Seabold, and S Gerber (2020). *Robert's rules of order newly revised.* PublicAffairs.

method is it can actually help you notice how you feel about something that may have been hard to put your finger on before. If you feel your heart sink when Tails shows up, then go with Heads!

❑ **Ranked Choice Voting/Instant Runoff Voting.** In this method, community members vote for their first, second, third choices, etc. If someone's first choice doesn't win, their second choice vote is counted. This works well when you have more than two options to vote on.

❑ **Proxy/Representative Voting.** This is where decision making is delegated to a smaller group of individuals (e.g., your finance committee is given power to make certain financial decisions on behalf of the community). This is a good choice if you don't want to overwhelm members with making decisions they do not want to be involved in, especially lower impact or technical decisions.

❑ **Sticky-dot Voting.** Options are posted and each person has three or five "dots" that they can use to indicate their top choices, with the top-voted options "winning." This is a good method if you are looking at choosing more than one option and also to get a sense of which options are most popular. Minority voters, however, may feel pushed out if none of their picks end up in the top three. When done synchronously, people may also be swayed to make choices based on where they see dots landing.

❑ **Weighted Voting.** If a decision will affect certain members of your community more than others, you may want to allow the affected members to have more say in the decision, such as by giving them two votes instead of just one.

❑ **Public Voting (Referendum).** Not exactly a decision-making process, but in certain instances you will need to decide whether votes are counted publicly (like a show of hands for who chooses the next speaker) or privately (via an online survey). Public voting is a quick method for low-stakes decisions, but is prone to people leaning towards others in their group, instead of voicing what may be their true feelings, so should be used with that caveat in mind.

These last two approaches are helpful if people are having trouble making a decision, or if you feel uneasy about the options you have.

❑ **Strategic Dissent.** Communities can fall into a pattern of "groupthink" where they don't push themselves enough to think outside the box. During discussions about an impending decision, it may be helpful to assign one or two people to intentionally provide counter arguments, as it can help lead groups to better decisions in the end.[40]

❑ **Three-way Decisions.** There may be times when it feels impossible to make a decision about something. In this case, it might work for your community to add a "third option," basically, instead of just "yes" or "no," also adding in "no opinion," or "decide later." The general advice here is that sometimes you may need to hold off and give yourselves more time to weigh other options or factors you need to consider.

We hope this list gives you a good start on some ideas about how to improve the overall decision-making strategy being used in your community. As you read through this chapter, did anything stand out to you that you are excited to try?

---

[40] This is known as a "devil's advocacy" technique in strategic decision-making.

NOTES

CHAPTER 16
Say "Yes, and…"

I used to supervise a group of Americorps VISTA members that changed over annually. These recent college graduates came onto our team full of enthusiasm and goals for the year. I had doubts about the scale and direction of some of their ideas, but I also felt like letting them try things out was a great way to keep them motivated, so I almost always gave them the green light, even when I felt nervous about whether it would really work. The vast majority of their projects were wildly successful, and as the years went by, I felt less and less anxious about giving them the go-ahead. —Eva

As Community Stewards, we often keep a lot of balls in the air. When someone walks in with an idea, it can feel like adding another ball to your juggling act, and quite possibly more than you feel you can handle. Similarly, as you start the process of decentralizing tasks and redistributing power, things can begin to feel chaotic and hard to manage, almost like they are out of your control.

To create a community that shares power, you'll need to acknowledge that the community knows what is best for itself, and step back to allow members to take initiative. This is actually harder than it sounds.

When a community member or group approaches you with an idea that makes your heart race, what's stopping you from encouraging them to run with it?

We propose using a strategy of saying, "Yes, and…". If this feels scary for you, remember that you're not just saying, "Yes." You're also saying "and…," which is crucial. Here are some ideas for how to make this strategy work for you:

❑ **Connect the proposed actions to actions or systems already happening in your community.** For example, say a member starts taking notes of a community meeting without asking permission from anyone. Say, "Yes, thank you! AND if you could put the notes in our shared document so everyone can access them and add to them, that would be awesome."

❑ **Be open to taking risks and learning.** Will one poorly coordinated event spell the end of your community? Unless your community is dealing with life or death issues, it's likely that even mistakes and missteps can support the learning of your community. Saying "Yes, and…" in situations where the impact of failure is not catastrophic is a great way to support members' self-determination and leadership capacity.

❑ **Make sure your "Yes, and…" is aligned with your community's expectations.** If in doubt about saying "Yes, and…", refer to your community's values, vision, and mission. For example, say a group of members want to organize a subgroup of "consultants for hire" under the banner of the community, and they have developed rules to determine who is in and who is out. You notice some of the rules they've proposed will marginalize certain groups of people in the community, and especially members who are already underrepresented in your community and domain area. Here's an important moment to focus on the "AND..." by stepping in to raise your concerns with the group.

❑ **Say more Yes's than No's.** Shutting down community members whenever they have a bright idea is only going to hurt your community. In fact, the more you say No, the more community members won't even bother asking anymore, and that's called disempowerment. We highly suggest that you save your No's for when you see a valid risk, a deviation from the community's mission, or something that might drive away members of the community.

Here are some questions to help you draw the line between "Yes" and "No":

→ Is the member volunteering to take on the bulk of the work of whatever they are suggesting?

→ Is the member proposing something that could possibly harm someone or something?

→ Is there anything in your mission, values, and principles that might be violated?

Even if the answers to these questions lead you towards a No, we suggest that you work with the member to understand together why their idea may be problematic. Then, try to find ways to adjust it together so it's a better fit for the community. The goal here is to uplift and encourage community members to step in, rather than deflate their efforts to be an active participant in the community.

"Yes, and..." is an easy way to loosen up power structures in your community. It helps members feel comfortable and welcome to jump into the community and act, and can have a galvanizing and energetic effect on everyone. If you've been struggling with getting more members actively involved in your community, here's your invitation to try out this simple "Yes, and..." approach.

NOTES

CHAPTER 17
Bring Your Community into Accounting Efforts

As a small business owner, every year I found my anxiety would rise during the weeks leading up to the tax filing deadline, because, frankly, my accounting was completely disorganized. Somehow I stumbled on Bari Tessler's book, "The Art of Money,"[41] and ended up taking her online course. I realized two very important things through her teaching: First, I gained a better understanding of how budgets and accounts work, which helped me feel less panicked about looking at numbers. Secondly, I realized I needed to hire an accountant for my business, because I just didn't want to have to deal with all those details. Both the clarity and especially the help from an accountant did wonders for alleviating my stress and helping me "keep my books clean," so that I now feel confident and clear about money going in and out. —Eva

There is nothing worse than feeling like you don't have a handle on your assets or liabilities. Regardless of whether your community collects money, operates with "tokens," or uses a "time-bank,"[42] creating even a simple accounting system that tracks assets coming in and going out can make a world of difference for your peace of mind and the well-being of the community.

Another important reason to clean up your accounting and open it to the community is because keeping your accounting secretive or only accessible to a few people can breed distrust and disempower members from feeling invested in fundraising and sustainability efforts.

In this chapter, we'll focus mostly on communities that are just getting started with their accounting.

If your community runs payroll, needs to pay taxes or receives grant funding, your accounting needs will be more complicated than what we're able to address here.

Here are some ideas to help you think through what you might want to include in your accounting so that it supports your community's path to being empowered and impactful. Remember, you may not need to do all of these things, and certainly not all at once. Work with your community to determine what will have the greatest impact, and start there.

❑ **Be transparent.** We want to emphasize how important transparency can be. Allowing your community to see your accounting practices and the numbers not only allows them to make

---

[41] Tessler, B (2016). The Art of Money: A Life-Changing Guide to Financial Happiness. Parallax Press.

[42] Some communities use tokens or timebanks to track contributions that volunteers make to the community. Tokens can be exchanged for services (e.g. I get 5 tokens for walking your dog, and can use those to "pay" another community member to water my garden), or included as part of members' responsibilities (e.g. all members must contribute 4 hours of volunteer time to the community each month).

better decisions about funding, but it can also contribute to their feeling of responsibility that the community remains financially healthy. This could mean making accounting documents public, providing regular updates at meetings, and/or sending out reports or account documents via your newsletter.

If you feel some resistance to this suggestion, we encourage you to dig into why. What about being transparent with your accounting makes you uneasy? What would you have to change to make you feel more comfortable sharing this information and responsibility?

❑ **Calendar it.** Let members know when they might expect updates on the budget. Is it monthly, quarterly, or annually? To meet these commitments, set aside time, put it in a schedule, and make sure that your accounting documents are as up-to-date as possible. If you are using a timebank or token system, make sure you give deadlines for members to update their numbers, so that everyone knows they are looking at the most recent balances.

❑ **Know how much money you have**. A chart of accounts is a common way to keep track of your money. Here's what it consists of:

→ **Assets:** These include cash in hand or owed to you, prepaid inventory (like a pile of t-shirts you plan to sell), and anything the community owns (like a computer or car).

→ **Liabilities:** These include credit card debt, any money you owe (including taxes), payroll or wages.

→ **Income:** This is money or resources that your community earns. For example, from sales or membership fees.

→ **Expenses:** This could be the cost of those t-shirts you bought with the plan to re-sell, supplies, rent, advertising fees, newsletter subscription services, and website hosting.

❑ **Use the resources around you.** If numbers and accounting aren't your superpower, look to your community for help. Chances are that there is someone within your group who is interested in taking a lead in this area. If not, consider hiring an accountant to at least get your books set up for you.

Automation can also help reduce your accounting burden. Most accounting platforms will allow you to connect your community's credit card or bank account to an accounting system, so that it automatically updates any time those accounts are used. Likewise, if you are using a membership management platform to collect fees, or a point-of-service app for collecting sales, you can hook those up into your software for easy updating.

❑ **Consider non-monetary costs and "in-kind" contributions.** If your community is largely volunteer-run, in-kind contributions may be really large, meaning that a lot of people are putting in a lot of time and effort to keep your community going. If you had to pay an hourly wage for these efforts, your community might not be able to afford to operate. In your chart of accounts, consider adding volunteer hours and accomplishments as income and expenses. Such accounting is especially helpful if you ever want to justify to a funder how much it actually costs to run your community.

❑ **Create a Budget**. A budget is an estimation or plan for what assets will be coming in to support the needs of your community. Because it is a prediction, it is useful to revisit the budget frequently to assess how reality is aligning with the actual numbers. You can decide to put a "cap" on certain expenditures, meaning that when all of one asset is used up, you can no longer spend out of that account. You can also adjust accounts by moving money from one account to another. The longer your community uses a budget, chances are that your predictions will become more accurate over time.

❑ **Set goals**. Setting fundraising or membership goals is an excellent way to motivate your community toward accomplishing a group effort. Particularly if you have a liability that you want to address, such as a loan you want to pay off, creating a plan and outlining how much income you need to bring in can help your community budget and set a direction for your income and asset-generation efforts. As with your chart of accounts or budgets, it is helpful to share the progress towards your goals with your membership regularly.

We recognize that setting up and monitoring accounting practices may sound tedious. But finances are key for sustaining any community. Bringing your community into the accounting and budgeting of the community can help members feel responsible and well informed about how to keep the community healthy.

NOTES

CHAPTER 18
Rethink the Language You Use

I am grateful that a colleague of mine introduced me to the title of "Facilitant," meaning, someone who facilitates a workshop or meeting, but also participates. I love this term because of the way it pulls the leader of the session down off of a podium and puts them into the crowd. I began introducing myself this way when appropriate, and would explain to the group that while I was leading the meeting, I was also participating. I found my brain worked really differently when I had the mindset that I could be in both roles simultaneously, and the title helped me maintain that mindset. —Eva

Language is powerful.

Let's say that again.

Language is powerful.

In our time working with leaders, facilitators, coaches, researchers, educators, and all types of communities, we have found many words that have jolted us out of our habitual ways of referring to ourselves and our collective work.

Being intentional with the terms can:

→ Shift power dynamics: Calling someone a "guide" rather than a "leader;"

→ Bring more clarity to a process: Calling it "knowledge-exchange" instead of "training;" or

→ Change the way people think about the community: Calling yourselves a "co-operative" instead of a "club."

As you read through the list of terms below, give yourself the opportunity to think more intentionally about the words that you currently use. Which terms might you want to change as you create and maintain a more empowered environment for your community?

We want to acknowledge that the exact origins of most of these terms are unknown to us. Some can be found in dictionaries (although perhaps with alternative meanings), while others were brought up in communities we've been a part of. This is also an invitation to you to invent words for your own community that more accurately describe the roles and ways of being you aspire to.

Here are some ideas to get you started:

❑ **Co - designer, conspirator, creator, etc.** We use "co-" to describe members who have created something in collaboration together. It can also be used to describe a collaborative process. For example, "Our governance model was co-designed by community members". This term is most powerful if it describes something that already occurred. If you use this term to signal an intention to bring everyone into the action, make sure that you can really deliver on it (e.g., have a collaborative process already designed), otherwise it can come across as inauthentic.

❑ **Collaborate.** Not to be confused with "working together," true collaboration occurs when people feel that they are equals. Collaboration among members is a key part of being a community.

- ❑ **Collective** and **Cooperative (or Co-op).** Both of these terms have action-oriented and in-stitutional underpinnings, and may be a better fit for your group than the word "community." Both strongly evoke the idea of shared power and authority. They also bring to mind a group that is working as activists/activators, such as "collective bargaining" within a union or a "food co-op" where bulk purchases made directly from farmers are shared amongst consumers.

- ❑ **Convener.** This is a good substitute for "leader." With this term, your role is focused on bringing people together. From there, the group can lead itself.

- ❑ **Facilitant.** a mashup of the words "facilitator" and "participant," this word gives a nod to the fact that we are a combination of leader and follower.

- ❑ **Guide.** This is another solid alternative for "leader," and is a title that can be given to many roles within your community. As a guide, one's role is to help members navigate, clear a path for easier participation, and model the way forward.

- ❑ **Host.** Like the Art of Hosting[44], we can all personify being a dinner host, even if it's not your dinner you are hosting.

- ❑ **Interdependent.** adrienne marie brown writes, "The idea of interdependence is that we can meet each other's needs in a variety of ways, that we can truly lean on others and they can lean on us."[45] Imagine working the term "interdependent" into your communications to describe how your community and its members operate.

- ❑ **Peer-Led.** If "peers" are equals, then inviting this term into your community helps set the tone that this is a level playing field. For example, you might be able to say: "Our group is a peer-led community for those interested in gaining a deeper understanding of…"

- ❑ **Steward.** As another alternative to "leader," a steward can be thought of less like a captain and more like a gardener, supporting the health and nourishment of the community so that it flourishes for the good of everyone who is a part of it. Stewards also strive to uplift community members, especially those with interest in leading.

- ❑ **We.** When we use the term "we" in our communities, especially in our written com-munications, we are immediately called to determine whether we are actually speaking for all members of the group. For example, "I believe that everyone should plant roses in their garden" versus "We believe that everyone should…" In this case, some people in your community may not agree with that statement, and wonder why you are attempting to speak on their behalf. Be careful not to weaponize "we" in order to wrestle people into a position or a perspective that they may not be comfortable with.

On the other hand, "I" versus "we" can be used to enhance feelings of shared ownership over outcomes. For example, saying "I would like to invite everyone…" versus "We would like to invite everyone…"

Using "we", as opposed to "you", also makes an author or speaker more accountable with what they are writing/saying. For example, "as part of our Code of Conduct, we commit to treating each other like…" versus "you commit to treating…"

As this list hopefully illustrates, choosing the words we use to describe our group, its members, or its activities is not something to be taken for granted. In fact, it may lead to some important discussions within your community, so that everyone can get on the same page about which terms they want to use, and why. You may even end up creating some new words just for your community.

Which of these might you start to incorporate? What other terms have you found useful for centering your community around its members?

---

44 Sandfort, J, N Stuber, and K Quick (2012). *Practicing the Art of Hosting*. University of Minnesota.
45 brown, a.m. (2017) *Emergent Strategy*. AK Press, page 87.

SECTION IV
COMMUNICATE CLEARLY

Reflect on this: The method, pace, and feeling of your communication is a reflection of who the community is and what it hopes to be.

As your community grows, you will likely find that the modes and volume of communication accelerates. Without thought and attention, communications can quickly spin out of control and become unmanageable and overwhelming (we're looking at you, 20-person chat thread!).

What might poor communication mean for your community?
→ People missing important announcements.
→ People not knowing key features of the community.
→ People confused about where to find information.
→ Conflicts and missed deadlines.

There are so many things that need to be communicated, from your community's mission, to member expectations, to upcoming events, to meeting minutes.

In this section we are taking a bird's eye view of your communications. Because communicating often feels like keeping multiple balls up at the same time, you may find it helpful to look at each piece of communication through five lenses: The Why, What, Who, How, and When.

1. The Why

The more clear you are about the reason for your communications, the more easily people will be able to process the information and enact your desired response. Some likely communication purposes include:

→ A Call to Action, by asking members to "Sign up now!" or "Click here!"
→ Share information, such as your community guidelines
→ Build relationships, like highlighting a member
→ Seek feedback, by asking members to complete a survey
→ Encourage engagement, by commenting on your own experience
→ Persuade, for example by explaining why a member should…

Reflect on your current communications and ask yourself: Do they all have a clear "Why?"

2. The What

The contents of your communications are likely varied, from things that require immediate action, to things that remain static for years. As you develop your content, keep in mind:

❑ **Be clear and concise**. Since everyone is inundated with communications, the more direct and easy-to-read each of your communications is, the more likely your message will be heard. A great role for a community member is to proof-read communications to make sure the messaging is understandable, that links work, and that important details (like dates and times) are correct.

❑ **Create rules of engagement and guidelines.** Set up a way for people to be aware of and agree to a set of standards before they participate, such as on social media groups and message boards. For example: "This platform is a hate-free space. Any perceived harassment or derogatory speech will be flagged, and may result in expulsion from the space. By checking this box, you are agreeing to communicate within our community guidelines."

The role of "moderator" is to ensure that your communications policy is being followed so the space remains useful and productive. If your community forums are very active, moderating can turn into a big but very important job.

❑ **Think about branding.** Branding determines your look, feeling, and includes your community's colors, shapes, font, and images. It helps people visually identify you among all of the other organizations and communities that exist. We recommend creating your branding early on so you can be intentional about how you want your community to be viewed.

3. The Who

Communications in a community is typically happening in many different directions, but you'll probably find that each piece of communications is directed to a specific audience. To help manage these different voices:

❑ **Identify your pathways.** Communications will likely come from and be received by: a) the "organization," which is represented by the people who speak on behalf of the overall community; b) groups of members; c) individual members; and d) people who are external to your community and may also be composed of different audiences (e.g., school teachers versus parents of students). The direction of your communications will either be internal-facing (within the community) or external-facing (outside the community).

❑ **Recruit people to help.** Communications can require a lot of work, but is also relatively easy to parcel out and decentralize across your community. You can create volunteer roles and committees that members can easily step into, such as Collaborative Workspace manager, blog editor, or video uploader.

❑ **Let people know how to update their info.** Give your members control over the information that is shared about them. Let members know how they can update their profile or their entry in the community directory.

4. The How

Most people already have ways that they like to communicate in their daily life. When joining a new community, they'd probably prefer to use the same platforms that they are already using, rather than learning how to use something new.

The best way to understand your audience and how they want you to communicate with them is to ask them!

5. The When

Once you've completed the breakdown of The Why, What, Who, and How, you can now turn this information into a full communications plan by establishing timelines and frequency for each type of communication.

❑ **Be consistent.** Communication works best when people know what to expect and when. Use a calendar to help your communications stay predictable for each piece of communication you've identified.

❑ **Keep a balance.** You'll want to strike a balance between overwhelming people with communications, and not communicating enough. For example, daily emails may go unread, while a Social Media presence that is only used once or twice a month might not register for people.

❑ **Learn from your data.** Learn from your community by noticing what gets traction, and what gets ignored. Keep an eye on your open rates for messages, your engagement rates on social media, and other metrics that can help you determine if you're doing too much, or not enough.

Remember, whatever you choose to emphasize will become an expected type of communication among the community–be careful you don't bite off more than you want to chew. If you are now realizing there's more on your plate than there needs to be, ask for help from the community or let your members know that a channel is going to be cut. It's OK to phase out a communication type or audience if you find it's no longer serving the broader community, or the effort is too high for the impact it's making. Make choices around where to prioritize your time and resources as you implement your communications strategy.

As you read through the rest of this section, notice which areas you feel excited about putting energy into, and start there.

NOTES

CHAPTER 19
Document, Document, Document

I recently took a sabbatical from the company I run. It didn't take me long to realize there were many things in my head that the group of people who would be running the company would need to know in my absence. With the help of a new project manager, we created an online document with links and a table of contents that could serve as a handbook/reference guide. It is something that I should have done long ago, but now that there was a group of people working on something that I had previously done on my own, it was absolutely essential. Like tossing out old clothes and organizing my closet, it was a breath of fresh air to see everything about the work clearly delineated and easy to access. —Eva

Do you ever feel like you're having the same meeting over and over again? Or maybe a leader within your community has stepped back, and now others are trying to figure out how to carry on the work without that member present. Worse, maybe someone is verbally harassing someone else in the community, and you say to them: Our community policies don't allow this type of behavior. But, oh no, your community has never written any such thing down before.

These are examples of why consistent and clear documentation is crucial to your overall communications strategy.

Documentation within your community means keeping a written record of progress—of decisions made, questions that have been answered, suggestions offered, credit due to specific individuals, final results and learnings, and next steps. Documentation is also key for helping everyone work in harmony together, so people aren't stepping on each other's toes, waiting for each other, or simply dropping the ball.

While all of this documentation may sound overwhelming, just remember that you can draw on the community to help. Afterall, these processes will likely include them, so who better than to test, read over, and revise them?

Documentation can take many different forms, each of which requires a slightly different strategy. Take a look below at some common types of documentation that are often part of communities, and see where your community might want to get more organized.

❏ **Keep meeting notes.** Meetings are where most collaboration occurs within communities, but being able to keep the momentum moving forward is where meeting notes come in.

Items to add to your meeting notes may include:

→ the date of the meeting

→ purpose/goals of the meeting

→ the people who attended

→ a tentative agenda

→ a summary of what was talked about in regards to each agenda item

→ any decisions that were made

→ action items with people's names assigned to them

If a meeting is part of a series of meetings that is generally attended by the same group of people, it can be easiest to keep all meeting notes on the same document (put the most recent meeting at the top). Such a rolling document structure helps to prevent unnecessary document proliferation. Otherwise, with all of the documentation that your community will likely create, you'll probably soon find that the number of documents begins to get out of control. This format also allows meeting attendees to refer to the previous meeting by simply scrolling further down in the document, so the meeting facilitator can more easily create the agenda based on the last meeting's action items and attendees can get quickly caught up.

❑ **Organize your documents.** Cloud-based storage, such as a Google folder, makes it easier for members to access and collaborate on documentation from anywhere at any time. Using this storage, you can maintain all of the files that are relevant to the community, and especially any documents, slide decks, or other products that were created collaboratively by the community.

To keep the structure of the files organized and intuitive to members, decide on a naming convention. For example, if you have a Communications committee, then anything that is created that falls under the topic of Communications should be filed under a folder called "Communications." Other folder categories might include Finance, Events, Board Meetings, etc.

If members are complaining about having trouble finding things, you may need to create a table of contents or a document that serves as an infrastructural map of the community's documentation, where the highest level topics (folders) are identified and defined, and then examples of activities that fit within this topic area are defined too.

Above all, stay as consistent as possible with how you name, organize, and set up each file. Don't forget to include a date, title, and authors— either in the file name or on the document itself.

❑ **Keep track of policies and guidelines.** Policies are the accumulation of decisions made in a community. They are typically drafted to summarize discussion and to "finalize" decisions so that everyone can get on the same page. They mark a point in time when decisions have been made, so that these same decisions and thoughts can be built upon and evolve as the community develops and matures. Some of the policies you will likely end up documenting in this way include:

→ How members join/leave

→ Expectations of members

→ Anything related to dues or fees

→ What to do if there is an incident with a member

→ Guidelines around communications like how to write Social Media posts

→ The process for appointing new volunteer leaders

Any existing policies should be made visible to members, such as by being displayed on the community website or by asking members to agree to them annually.

❑ **Capture your procedures and workflows.** In contrast to policies, procedures document the details of how things get done. They are often created through discussion and trial and error of what is working and not working, and may be changed without much formal agreement from the community.

By documenting a procedure, a new volunteer community member (or staff member) can easily step into an activity and hit the ground running. Some common workflows for a community may be:

→ How to review the application of a new member

→ How to write a community newsletter

→ How to host and organize the monthly seminar

Some of your procedures may be more administrative, and require more attention to ensure that they are being done consistently in alignment with existing laws and fiduciary requirements. Here are some areas of administration that might benefit from an established procedure:

→ **Bookkeeping.** This includes how you invoice and collect membership dues, how bills are paid, how your reconcile payments, and how financial data are organized.

→ **Hiring.** This includes how employees are paid, how you decide to hire people, and contract templates.

→ **Equipment use and maintenance.** If you have shared equipment, you'll need to document any protocol for use, what to do if the equipment breaks, and who decides what equipment to purchase.

→ **Online platforms.** Document user names and access to platforms, how to handle two-factor authentication and ownership succession, and how to ensure security of your systems.

If you find yourself with a growing collection of documented procedures, consider creating handbooks so users can find information more quickly. For example, you may want to have a Handbook for Organizing Events that outlines what a person in charge of an event needs to do. It might contain sections on how to get budget approval, how to reserve event locations, or where to get posters printed. A Handbook for New Members might include a list of important dates, contact lists, and/or your community's policies.

❑ **Use Project Management Spreadsheets** (Table 19.1). Think of these spreadsheets as a "to do" list for any larger initiatives and events. Typically, you'll want to track a) what the task is, b) who will do the task, c) by when the task needs to be completed, d) status of the task, and e) any other notes that are relevant. Here's what a basic spreadsheet might look like:

Table 19.1. An example of a spreadsheet for managing a collaborative effort.

What	Who	When	Status	Notes
Draft donation letters	Mani	By Oct 4	Not yet started	Remind team to add to the list of potential donor organizations
Calculate costs for workshop	Sandra	Oct 7	Done	Look at last year's budget

❑ **Remember to "Version" your documentation.** To make sure everyone is using the latest, most updated document, add an indicator of their "version," which is typically a date and the names of people who updated it. Versioning means that you know that there is always potential for a better version of a policy or a workflow, since things always change based on context and our own maturity of knowledge.

By keeping clear documentation, community members can easily step into and out of activities.

They'll also have a better idea of what is expected in the community.

As a bonus, if your community ends up receiving governmental grants or funding, these documented policies and procedures are also the types of things that financial auditors will ask to see. If you are feeling like your current documentation may not be as robust or organized as you'd like it to be, now might be the time to revisit your strategy.

NOTES

CHAPTER 20
Articulate Your Values, Vision, Mission, and Goals

At the end of a recent all-day weekend strategic planning retreat, one participant told me that they had been dreading the boredom and frustration they were sure they would face at the meeting. Yet, they were surprised at how quickly the time flew by, and how inspired they felt by the vision, values and mission their group had developed.

As a process facilitator for strategic planning and retreats, I have had the honor of witnessing firsthand as groups come together to put their finger on exactly what it is they are hoping to accomplish as a community. One of my most favorite moments as a facilitator is the palpable sense of relief and forward momentum that the group feels at the end of our time together, when they can look proudly at the clearly stated set of values, vision, mission and goals that they just co-created. I leave those sessions feeling confident and happy that the group will be able to accomplish great things together, now that they are all on the same page and have a plan in hand. —Eva

One of the first things you communicate to the world is who you are as a community, including what you stand for, what you do, and what you hope to achieve. A community can come into conflict or run into issues like declining membership, lack of participation, and waning impact when these values, vision, missions, and goals are not clear, collectively surfaced, agreed upon, and widely broadcast.

Throughout this guide, we seed you with a few different values–like sharing power, creating a sense of belonging, and centering wellness. We hope that all Community Stewards reading this book would aspire to these values. But these are *our* values, not yours or ones your community has developed. So it's time to get yours down on paper (or revisit them!), if you haven't already, so you can communicate them out to the world.

Below, we define what each of these pieces of your identity means, and offer some examples for you to reflect upon.

❑ **Values**. These are the underlying ethics, beliefs, and ideals that your community is built upon. Values statements often begin with the phrase, "In our community, we believe that…" We're guessing that right now you can probably rattle off a number of your community's values, even if you've never thought of it that way before. As a steward, you need to:

→ Help your community collectively define what its values are.

→ Continuously communicate those values.

→ Make sure that decisions made for the community are always in line with its values.

Here is an example of values from the National Parent Teacher Association (PTA)[46]:

→ **Collaboration:** *We will work in partnership with a wide array of individuals and organizations to broaden and enhance our ability to serve and advocate for all children and families.*

→ **Commitment:** *We are dedicated to children's educational success, health, and well-being through strong family and community engagement, while remaining accountable to the principles upon which our association was founded.*

→ **Diversity:** *We acknowledge the potential of everyone without regard, including but not limited to: age, culture, economic status, educational background, ethnicity, gender, geographic location, legal status, marital status, mental ability, national origin, organizational position, parental status, physical ability, political philosophy, race, religion, sexual orientation, and work experience.*

→ **Respect:** *We value the individual contributions of members, employees, volunteers, and partners as we work collaboratively to achieve our association's goals.*

→ **Accountability:** *All members, employees, volunteers, and partners have a shared responsibility to align their efforts toward the achievement of our association's strategic initiatives.*

❑ **Vision**. This is your chance to do some big picture thinking and even some reach-for-the-stars dreaming. Ask yourselves: If your community were 100% successful in its mission, what would the world be like? Creating a vision is extraordinarily helpful for a community because it gives everyone a "north star" to work towards. For example, if your vision is a neighborhood where everyone has access to a garden plot, can you imagine some of the actions your community might take to make that happen? Developing a vision makes decision-making a lot easier as you continuously ask, "Does this activity help us move in the direction of our vision?"

❑ **Mission**. Have you heard of an elevator pitch? You know, the one impactful sentence that you can tell someone about yourself or your community in the time it takes to ride up in an elevator? That's what a mission statement is. It succinctly describes who and where you serve, why you do what you do, and what it is that you do. Being clear with your mission helps members–and the world at large–understand what you are about. It is often the first thing people see on your website. In addition to helping you make decisions (does this meet our mission or not?), a mission statement can also help you attract new members, funding, and other resources.

Here are some examples of mission statements:

Boys and Girls Clubs of America: "To enable all young people, especially those who need us most, to reach their full potential as productive, caring, responsible citizens."

"The mission of the World Wildlife Fund is to conserve nature and reduce the most pressing threats to the diversity of life on Earth. Our vision is to build a future in which people live in harmony with nature."

"Here at Costco, we have a very straightforward, but important mission: to continually provide our members with quality goods and services at the lowest possible prices."

---

[46] National Parent Teacher Association (n.d.) Mission Statement. www.pta.org/home/About-National-Parent-Teacher-Association/Mission-Values.

❑ **Goals.** Goals change over time, so it is helpful to revisit them at least once a year, if not more often. They are generally thought of in phases, such as "short term" and "long term." Once you've identified your goals, you can use them to create an Action Plan that defines the steps towards reaching each goal including who, how, and when.

It can be tempting to skip the step of creating values, a vision, mission, and goals in community stewardship because it is much more fun to get to the "being" and "doing" parts of community work.

You might also feel like your community isn't "ready" to figure it all out. However, without clarity and commitment to your identity, it's easy to lead yourself astray with misaligned decision-making, out-of-scope work, and uncoordinated efforts. It's perfectly OK to treat these elements of your community as a work in progress. In fact, it's likely that these things will change as your community deepens its identity.

If you are feeling stuck and unsure of where to start, use Table 20.1 to create a rough outline of a mission statement to get the ball rolling.

Table 20.1. Template for developing an outline for a mission statement.

Question to reflect upon	Your response in the context of your community
Who does your community serve?	
Where does your community serve?	
What do you do?	
Why do you do what you do?	

Once you have your mission, vision, values, and goals outlined (The What), take some time to think about how you can keep what you've agreed on alive in your community (The How and When) by communicating them, and bringing them into the work that you do. These are now your guideposts for all of your activities. How will you keep them central in your community?

NOTES

CHAPTER 21
Outline Expectations

Before I start any meeting, I take a moment to review Community Agreements[47], guidelines, or intentions, all of which are ways of looking at how the group expects to work together and behave during the meeting. I've found that if I don't do this, people start doing things I'd never expect, like forgetting to mute themselves during a virtual meeting as they walk into a cafe to order coffee. A simple, "Keep yourself on mute when you're not talking," would really help with these situations. —Eva

Every space we enter is permeated with a set of expectations. Think about how you behave when you walk into a dentist's office versus when you walk into your own home. On any given day, we pass through dozens of different environments, and in each one, whether we're aware of it or not, we adjust our behavior.

Even if you don't think your group holds expectations or you haven't named any yet, you can be 100% sure each person holds an idea of how they should behave when they're participating in your community. If you aren't clear about defining and communicating what the collective expectations are, conflict and confusion will eventually ensue.

There are many reasons why clear and transparent expectations for communities are important:

→ They help members decide if the community is a good fit for them.

→ They get people on the same page about the rules of membership, thus reducing potential conflict between members.

→ They help members feel empowered. By knowing where the guardrails are, members are more confident about acting within them and making decisions that are inline with community expectations.

→ They help avoid insider culture when only a certain set of people are aware of the rules. Such transparency is particularly important if your community is diverse (e.g., different age groups, cultural backgrounds, professional domains), since misunderstandings may arise more easily.

These types of expectations are often called things like community agreements, guidelines, norms, rules, terms, code of conduct, and "ways of being in community together." We are pretty sure you've come across these written expectations many times in various contexts before.

For empowered and impactful communities, community expectations usually have three elements in common:

1. They are formalized by being written down.

---

[47] See the chapter about "community agreements" in Meyers, EJ (2019) *Raise the Room: A Practical Guide to Participant-Centered Facilitation.* Spark Decks. Pages 77-79

2. Community members, who are the people who are affected by the expectations, have played a role in developing them and agree on them.

3. They are a "living document," meaning they are used, questioned, and updated frequently. In this way, community expectations change as the membership changes, and as the community and society around it evolves.

You can also think of community expectations as existing at two different scales:

→ **High-level.** These are the types of expectations that are used to guide the entire community. Such expectations are thoughtfully developed and reviewed by as many people from the community as possible. One example of this is a "Member Terms/Agreements"[48], which are particularly relevant for communities that have a formal way of determining members (e.g., membership application or fees). Members will also need to agree on these high level expectations regularly, such as during membership renewal or other milestone events when the full community comes together.

→ **Contextual.** These types of expectations are developed for specific contexts, such as in Eva's story when she is hosting a meeting or in certain locations like in the bathroom where you might find a sign reminding you, "Paper towels are made from trees, take only what you need."

As you develop or revise your community expectations, there are a number of strategies that are helpful to keep in mind:

❑ **Aim for higher level principles, and then provide examples to clarify**. "Strive to always make everyone feel welcomed," may be the expectation, while examples of this may be, "Say hello to anyone who comes through our door, ask people how you can be helpful, and offer resources." A great way to help make these clear is to ask community members to contribute their own examples of what a given expectation means to them.

❑ **Set your expectations in positive, rather than in negative language.** A fun example is "Don't run in the hallways," which may lead to people skipping, riding their bicycles, or sprinting (I'm not running, I'm "sprinting!"). Instead, be clear about what you DO want to see, such as by saying "We walk in the hallways." It is much easier for us to follow positive rules.

❑ **Be aware that terms can have more than one meaning.** People have different backgrounds, life experiences, and blind spots. What may be an innocent term to you, may be a loaded or confusing term for someone of another culture.

A classic example is "Be respectful." While lovely in concept, not everyone has experienced this phrase in a positive way. For example, more powerful groups have often weaponized the phrase to assert their place in social hierarchy and shut down voices from historically marginalized groups. Opening up a discussion, offering examples, or asking people to help come up with a new way of describing the term can help everyone get on the same page. Check in with your community, and especially with historically marginalized members, to hear about how different terminology may sound to them.

Once you've developed your community expectations, how do you implement them? The last thing you want to do is spend a lot of time and energy "policing" your members. If you find that expectations are continuously being ignored or broken by your members, it may be time to revisit those expectations to see if the problem is that they are out of alignment with what your community needs. We suggest that you focus the majority of your attention on helping community members meet expectations by doing the following:

---

[48] A Member Terms/Agreement articulates the rules and policies around membership, including when/how membership is renewed, criteria for membership, and any actions that would lead to termination from the group. To activate this document, a member must formally agree to it when they become a member. You'll need to check with a legal professional to ensure that none of your membership rules conflict with state or federal laws.

❑ **Ensure everyone knows the expectations.** We have a lot on our minds, and it can be hard to remember which communities we belong to are connected with which expectations. To keep them alive, you'll need to share them among the community as often as you can. State them up front before meetings or events, introduce them to new members before they join, and post and highlight them where they're easy to find.

❑ **Be consistent.** Your expectations and agreements apply to everyone, AND each of them needs to make sense with all of your other expectations or agreements. For example, if your mission is about equity and accessibility, then it wouldn't make sense for the community to hold events in spaces that are not wheelchair accessible.

Of course the worst can happen, and you might have a member who fails to meet expectations. If that does happen, you'll need to have a protocol for what to do when expectations are not being met by a member. In the final section of this guide we go into more depth about how to handle incidents within your community, including what to do when an agreement gets broken.

Being intentional, transparent, and consistent with expectations is key for building trust in a community, so everyone knows what is acceptable and what isn't. If you haven't yet worked with your community to develop a set of expectations, or if your expectations are not known to all members, now is the time to start the conversation by asking: "What do we expect of ourselves, as members of this community?" You may be surprised at how aligned you already are.

NOTES

CHAPTER 22
Improve Your Virtual Infrastructure

I was recently helping a new community develop their online presence. I thought it would be easy since it had been only a year ago when I'd gone through a similar process with another community. But when I began signing them up for my go-to platforms for event organizing and newsletters, I found that many of the platforms now had pretty restrictive free accounts or pricey paid accounts. As a new emerging community that was still exploring its value to its members, it didn't make sense to start expanding their budget from the get-go. I had to invest substantial time in assessing new platforms, and learning how to use them. — Arika

While we might think of the heartbeat of our community as happening when we get together over a picnic or in-person event, almost all communities today use virtual tools[49] to connect, communicate, and ultimately drive their mission forward. These tools have the capacity to make our community more productive and efficient, but it can be confusing to navigate which tools to use because there are so many options out there and the landscape is always changing. Likewise, familiarity and understanding of how to use the tools may vary amongst community members, causing some to feel "out of the loop," frustrated, and disconnected.

If you've got a fully online community, we can't emphasize enough the importance of having a dedicated person or group that keeps an eye on the virtual infrastructure of the community. Such attention can make or break your community by making sure that the community can quickly evolve and pivot with technology, so your community isn't suddenly left in the cold when a platform raises its prices or goes out of business.

Choosing virtual tools that are overly complicated— or choosing too many tools—can confuse members,

so taking the time to think through your options and vet them through your members is essential. Do most people in your community have a smartphone, tablet, or personal computer? Consider what sorts of tools your community is more likely to be using, and, if you don't know, ask them!

As Arika described in her story above, the technological landscape changes quickly. Throughout this guide we generally steer away from listing specific tools and focus instead on the broader categories of platforms, so what we write here will stand the test of time. In this chapter, however, we do mention specific tools that are currently popular to give you an example of the type of tool we are talking about.

The list of tools that we include in Table 22.1 is by no means exhaustive, but rather, an introduction to some of the most common technical solutions that are used by communities to stay organized and communicate effectively. We encourage you to dig a little deeper into the features of different platforms that peak your interest, so you can build and design easier ways for your community to communicate and collaborate.

---

[49] Virtual tools are interchangeably known as "online," "digital," or "web-based" tools, platforms, or software.

Table 22.1. Types of virtual tools used to support community stewardship and their pros and drawbacks.

Type and Description	Pros	Drawbacks
Messaging App These are things like SMS group texts, WhatsApp, and Telegram, which are generally cell phone based.	→ Reach people quickly and consistently. → Good for sharing information, like photos, between a few people and for weighing in on topics that are fairly straightforward and short-term ("Anyone available to meet at the park tomorrow?"). → Some communities rely on their phones as their primary technological tool, and this type of communication can literally be a life saver for them.	→ Some people might be less inclined to participate in messaging app-based groups because the deluge of messages can be invasive and overwhelming. → Threads or more complex discussions are difficult to do on these platforms.
Social Media or Social Networks Social Media are platforms primarily used for sharing content, for example, X (Twitter), Bluesky, YouTube, and Instagram. In contrast, Social Networks are primarily spaces that support interactions between people. Some examples of social networks are LinkedIn, Facebook, and NextDoor. Many social media and social networks overlap, although most platforms lean more heavily towards one or the other.	→ Easy to connect with a large group of people, and especially to build relationships with strangers.	→ It can be challenging to get past a superficial level of "knowing" people. → There is typically only one main "channel" for people to communicate with each other, so conversations that include more than a few people or topics can get confusing fast.
Collaborative Workspaces Platforms like Slack and Discord allow you to create smaller sub-groups (or channels) so that community members can interact in the sub-groups that are most important to them. Private messaging between small groups is also possible.	→ With these workspaces, it's possible to create a complex layered structure that mimics the nuances of a community. → Members can create their own channels, allowing communities to self-organize. → These platforms are best for communities that are highly active and collaborating in small teams on different projects. → These workspaces can be used to effectively and quickly share updated information, workflows, and policy changes across a community.	→ It can be difficult to discover new channels. → If people aren't used to using workspaces, they can forget to check in and use it. → People who aren't as comfortable with technology may be reluctant to join yet another new platform that is outside of their typical workflow. → In really active communities, information can be ephemeral and fast-moving.

Type and Description	Pros	Drawbacks
Community Management Platform These platforms can be a great choice for paid membership communities. They provide all-in-one services, so membership renewal, content, courses, and events can all occur in one place. Some examples of these are Mighty Networks, Wild Apricot, Join It, and Circle.	→ One of the best features about these platforms is that all of the information for a community is in a single place. This makes it easier for the Community Steward to set up the community and manage it.	→ These platforms require a monthly subscription that can be pricey for many communities. → Having all of your community content and tools hosted in one place can impact your community's flexibility. For example, in the case that the platform suddenly raises its prices, or worse decides to close, you may find it very difficult to move everyone to a new platform. → As with the Collaborative Workspaces, some potential members may be reluctant to join a new platform that is only used for your community.
Listserv or Newsletters A Listserv is a mailing list that people can join to both send and receive emails from a group of people, as well as look back at an archive of message threads to see what they missed. A Newsletter is one-directional, providing a centralized way for a leadership team to communicate with and hold a community together.	→ Listservs are a good choice for people who are primarily email-based, and for groups that don't send out frequent messages. → Listservs and newsletters are archived, so what you write becomes a historical and published record about your community that people can refer to. → Newsletters provide an overarching hub to summarize what's going on in the community, and how the community works. → Listservs and Newsletters provide a function for people to subscribe/unsubscribe from your emails.	→ Some listservs can create an overwhelming volume of email. → Our inboxes are often inundated with newsletters from various companies and organizations, so a community newsletter may be easily overlooked.
Online Forums If you are looking for a web-based version of a bulletin board, this is for you. Some examples of community online forums are Discourse and Stack Overflow.	→ Out of all of the platforms listed in this category of infrastructure, these forums offer the most persistent form of communication within a community. For this reason, these forums are most often used to help support technical or software development, since they can be searched by someone who has a problem that's likely been solved by someone else.	→ Forums are often not that conducive for collaboration, since they are clunky to use for fast, real-time interaction.

Type and Description	Pros	Drawbacks
Meeting Platforms Most communities need a way to communicate via a video-based platform. Popular meeting platforms like Zoom, Google Hangouts, and Facetime allow people to have video conferences and chat with others at the same time. Interactive meeting platforms like Kumospace and Gather.town allow people to virtually move an avatar around a space and have video conferences with individuals and groups.	→ Allow people to meet from their home or office, without having to travel to a destination.	→ Meeting platforms are a ubiquitous part of most people's personal and working lives, but not everyone may be as comfortable communicating or navigating through the software. Unstable or limited internet connection can really hamper people's access.
Websites Websites provide a home for a community that is controlled entirely by your community.	→ You can be sure that no one is taking and selling your data (like many social media and social network platforms do), and you won't be surprised by a corporate takeover.	→ Websites require dedicated energy to update, we suggest that websites contain long-lasting ("evergreen") information like your mission statement or list of board members, while using other online platforms for information that changes more often.
Event Manager Platforms Tools like a Google Calendar, Facebook Events, LinkedIn Events, or Eventbrite can help your community know what event is coming up next, who is planning to attend, and important information about the event.	→ Using the same designated platform for your events help you record your virtual sessions, see who registered and attended, and collect people's contact information. → These platforms can send out automated email reminders and notifications to registrants, making the job of an event coordinator easier. → If your community is spread out geographically, these platforms can help you avoid time zone mishaps when getting events on people's calendars.	→ Some of these platforms charge a fee that can get expensive if you have a lot of users.

Type and Description	Pros	Drawbacks
Collaboration Productivity Suites Examples are the Google suite and Microsoft teams that have sets of tools that allow people to collaborate via shared documents, slide decks, spreadsheets, and whiteboards.	→ Using these tools, community members can collaborate to create documentation of policies, workflows, and records of meetings in a centralized cloud-based storage space that is accessible to all contributors or designated users.	→ These documents are often owned by an individual (perhaps you), who can easily remove members' access to documents. If that person leaves the community under disgruntled circumstances, the community could lose access to all of their important documents (recommendation: make backups!).
Repositories and Libraries If your community produces public-facing content like white papers or slide decks, you'll need a place to put them. Platforms like Zenodo and Figshare provide a place where documents can be publicly deposited for the intention of persisting over the long term. They are provided with a Digital Object Identifier (DOI), which helps a document get discovered, more easily cited, and indexed with search engines like Google.	→ These platforms are a great place to point to when you need to share about your value with funders. Repositories are useful for ensuring that finalized community resources are always available to members, whether or not they continue to be a part of the community.	→ For more informal communities, a document repository is probably not needed.

As you read through these options, which ones seem like they might be a good addition to your communication strategy? Where are you experiencing the most friction in your community right now, and which tool might be able to help?

NOTES

CHAPTER 23
Acknowledge People for their Contributions

In one community that I was a part of, every time we created a community document (a document that was created and/or vetted by the community), we wrote up a paragraph about the development of that document. This paragraph consisted of the names of people who created the first draft, contributed revisions to the document itself, and attended specific meetings to add input, as well as the dates and places that these things happened. I believe that such transparency is important for defining what it means when something has been "developed by the community." It also acknowledges the ever changing composition of a community, and gives a nod to people who left their mark on the community in fundamental ways. Years down the road, it made it easier to follow up on documents and get a better sense of the thinking behind it. — Arika

Recognizing and thanking people for contributing to the development and well-being of the community is a powerful tool. Communities can sometimes feel like an entanglement of individuals, where it is hard to separate out who has contributed to what. The truth is, individual *people*–and not the community entity itself–create things on behalf of the community. Being honest and authentic about this simple fact can go a long way in helping members feel both valued and impactful with their contributions.

Figuring out who to recognize and how to communicate that recognition in a community, however, is harder than it seems. Here are some common issues:

→ **The number of thank yous can be overwhelming.** If you try listing all of the people who have done something valuable for the community, it's likely that you're going to leave someone out.

→ **You may not be aware of all of the contributions.** When you publicly thank specific people for their "service" to the community, you will likely be missing those who are doing under-the-radar types of contributions, like consistently answering questions on a forum, or organizing a closet that's been neglected for years.

→ **Thanking people can create a dynamic of reliance on external motivation.** If you make a habit of thanking people for things they already enjoy doing, you may create a transactional environment for community service. In other words, people may feel the absence of a thank you when you *don't* offer external motivation, which could lessen their desire to take action in the future.

→ **The balance between "we" and "I" can get out of whack.** The last thing you want to have happen as you offer your gratitude is to create a competitive environment. For example, did you ever have to do a group project for school? Did everyone pull equal weight in that project? It can feel terrible to someone who has put a lot of work into something individually to only be recognized collectively. On the flip side, to only recognize one person within a group of people who contributed equally may also foster hard feelings.

The bottom line is that when you–as a Community Steward–express gratitude at a community-level, you run the risk of creating a problem that didn't exist before. But what kind of community would we be stewarding if we were discouraged (or too afraid) to credit and communicate gratitude to each other?

Here are a few of our thoughts on how to handle acknowledgements on behalf of the community:

❑ **Thank people for the roles they play.** As a Community Steward, you have a responsibility to the community as an entity. Part of that responsibility is recognizing the effort that community members put into serving the community organizationally. Focusing on people who hold specific roles in the community is one way to easily determine when someone should be thanked publicly. Examples of this might be members of the Board of Directors or Advisory Board, and specific leads of a group–basically any formal role in the community that has a name.

❑ **Make sure you thank everyone involved.** There is a delicate balance between assuming that one person was more responsible than others in accomplishing something, and glossing over an individual's contributions by generalizing them into a group. For example, when it was actually one person who did most of the work on a project, you could say "A big thank you to Zara for leading the project, and the other members of the Membership committee for their support," instead of saying "Thanks to the Membership committee!".

❑ **Thank people "off of the podium."** You, as an individual community member, are encouraged to thank anyone you want on a personal level. It may, however, be helpful to let people know that these thank yous are coming from the place of being a community member, not leader. For example, you may want to use your personal email, rather than a community-identified email address or signature, for these types of messages.

❑ **Thank people at milestone moments.** The end of the year or at an annual meeting are times that many communities offer gratitude for the successes of individuals and teams. When someone leaves a formal role within a community (e.g., your fundraising chair steps down), summarize what they accomplished and offer your appreciation. Likewise, any time that someone leads the completion of a project or product is a great time to recognize and thank them.

❑ **Give back with written words.** A thoughtful gift is always appreciated, but so are thoughtful words, especially if they are written down so that someone can come back to them and re-read them later. For more visible thank yous, consider putting your words of gratitude into a regular place for community communication like your monthly newsletter or Collaborative Work-space. This also implies that you should have a section or channel for where these types of announcements go.

❑ **Credit people.** Depending on the type of community you are stewarding, there may be opportunities to highlight the contributions and accomplishments of members that goes beyond showing gratitude. For example, your writing group may acknowledge every time someone publishes an article or book; or your gardening club might want to amplify members who receive awards at the local county fair for their floral arrangements.

You are encouraged to always credit people for things that they've done, and especially if it went beyond the typical commitment and time that most people put into a community. For example, "Eugenia and Adrian took the lead on writing the first draft of our membership policy."

We can also think of crediting as "attribution", which is the ability to trace back to the sources of where a product came from. This is important for understanding the broader context of a product, including what influenced the development of a product and what perspectives were provided or might be missing.

In some formal settings, like article publishing, there are guidelines that are used by professional societies and journals to decide who should be credited for writing and acknowledged for contributing to an article. Your community can adopt and develop similar guidelines to help decide who gets recognized and how. Such guidelines can help you and others be consistent around how you thank and credit people in the community. By being consistent, you can better protect yourself from your own biases regarding who you notice, and worse, who you don't notice.

Now that you've read through these options, where might you want to offer gratitude or acknowledge people's contributions?

NOTES

CHAPTER 24
Share Everyone's Successes

One of the most wonderful things about communities is that we get to share in each other's successes. If you have cultivated an abundance mindset within your group, one member's success is the success of the community, and vice versa. It's a mutually beneficial and uplifting dynamic.

In a more pragmatic sense, members' successes also allow the community to exponentially produce "outputs" with relatively minimal investment. Just think: If you've got 100 members and each one contributes one output every few months—say a blog post, a recorded presentation, or another personal achievement that contributes to the mission of the community, then the community has succeeded in creating over 400 products a year!

Anyone can see that there can be great benefit to designing a system for this community-sourcing effort. Even if we hired a team of employees to try to produce this many wins, would they come up with the same level of diversity of outputs and breadth of expertise that a community could?

So, here's the catch: How do we capture all of this output?

Below is a list of suggestions for how to gather together the wins of the community. The list is generally arranged from more to less frequent activities. For example, self-reporting can happen on a daily basis, while video recordings and blog posts might happen on a monthly basis. We've also noted if items are outward-facing (directed to the general public) or internal-facing (directed to the community).

☐ **Share on Social Media** (outward-facing). It doesn't take much effort to encourage people to post their successes on their personal Social Media or other public venues. Your challenge here is to gather this information together on behalf of the community, and push it along in a coordinated workflow. One way is to ask members to tag the community organization in a post when it's relevant. Or, you could have a volunteer look out for these posts, and then share them on the community Social Media or another internal medium (see the next item).

☐ **Set up a system for personal achievements reporting** (internal-facing). This is a crowd-sourced way for community members to self-report their successes. Most people like sharing their successes, so this is a really easy one that takes minimal administrative work. All you have to do is figure out a good venue for people to use, and get people into a habit of using it.

☐ **Capture video recordings** (outward-facing). Does your community host presentations by members?

If so, you'll want to do your best to record these and post them on Social Media, and especially those that cater specifically to videos. One rule of thumb with these recordings is to get permission to share the video publicly from every single person who is featured. You can imagine that this would be pretty problematic for discussion-based events. To keep it simple (and avoid conflicts) you can focus on recording presentations featuring a few people who have prepared a talk beforehand, like a seminar. Note that these video recordings can also be made "internal" (if presenters don't wish the recording to be made public) and become part of your in-house learning library.

❑ **Host a blog** (outward-facing). Community members will often want to have a voice in the community—a place to share their personal thoughts and stories. Providing an outward-facing blog, and a process for people to submit blog posts, is a great way to do this. While this might sound daunting from an administrative perspective, it's actually a great fit for a team of volunteers to do since it's a pretty tightly scoped activity. Just be sure to clarify the scope of the blog and expectations around content, such as by creating Blog Guidelines.

❑ **Establish a Repository** (outward-facing). This can be used to collect slide decks and other written products that are created by the community or by individuals in the community. The best platforms to use also offer a DOI (Digital Object Identifier) for these products. A DOI is used in today's world to support archiving and discovery of outputs—much like a global library code. As an added benefit, such publications are often considered formal products that can be reported to funders.

❑ **Send out a newsletter** (outward and internal-facing). Newsletters are a way to gather a summary of the community's successes into one place, so you can communicate these with a wider audience, such as your mailing list of supporters who are not necessarily members. Be aware that it can take quite a bit of work to create a newsletter; if your newsletter is volunteer-run, it's often realistic to aim for producing these about once a quarter.

❑ **Pull together and share an end-of-the-year report** (outward-facing). This report is used to pull together all of the highlights of the community over the past year. It can take different forms, like a blog post, slide deck, or white paper. While it does sound like a lot of effort, it can be incredibly useful for tracking how the community is doing, celebrating successes with the community, and providing a quick snapshot of the community that you can point to when you need to justify the existence or continued existence of the community (funding anyone?). If you've done a good job implementing some of the aforementioned ideas, then an end-of the-year report is not such a heavy lift.

As an additional note, here's a conundrum to consider: What do you do about a member's achievement that you personally don't like very much? For example, an article that was poorly written and filled with grammatical errors, or a perspective that you don't agree with (provided it doesn't violate any of your community ethics policies). You celebrate it anyway! If you feel that the product reflects poorly on your community, then you should probably re-examine your membership or communications policy. You should be prepared to support and celebrate ALL of your members in a consistent way.

To get started on sharing the successes of your community, try implementing just one or two methods and sticking with it until it feels well-embedded in the community. It can also be beneficial to offer opportunities for members to share what they've learned or appreciated from seeing these successes. Was there something that helped them make a leap or tackle a problem they were facing? Was there something that they related to on a personal level? Gathering feedback on the successes you've shared can help you figure out what method to try next.

SECTION V
BE READY FOR ROUGH WATERS

Reflect on this: We cannot anticipate every twist and turn that gets thrown in our community's way. What we CAN do is prepare ourselves for when the unexpected occurs.

We never want to have to deal with incidents, conflicts, or negative feelings within a community, but with a large group of people interacting together it's unavoidable. Issues will arise and catch us off guard. It's tough, but as a Community Steward, it's often your role to address uncomfortable situations head-on and lead the group towards a healthy resolution—one that aligns with the values and mission of the community.

Naturally, when something isn't feeling good, our "fight or flight" response kicks in. We might dig in our heels and try to fix the situation quickly and forcefully, such as by shutting down a chat thread that was causing the argument. Or, we might do what we can to put some space between ourselves and that negative feeling, like ignoring a visible conflict between two people and hoping it goes away on its own. Sadly, these responses, made in the heat of the moment, often have negative consequences that harm the community further.

To better prepare yourself and your community for those unexpected incidents, we can turn towards the experiential learning cycle[50]. In short, experiential learning encourages us to reflect on what happened, develop a theory of what we could do differently to get a better result, and then test out our hypothesis. By using the cycle, we focus on learning from what happened, which will help us feel better prepared for the next time we are in a similar situation.

To make the most out of experiential learning, we encourage you to:

❑ **Schedule time for it**. After your community has experienced something new, schedule a call to debrief with community members to improve your understanding of what happened from different perspectives. Or, build this reflection time into an existing meeting by adding it as an agenda item.

❑ **Reflect on feedback**. In communities, any criticisms offered are often done out of the general interest and engagement from a member. When you hear critical comments, it can be hard not to take it personally, but we encourage you to pause and reflect on it. Try responding with, "Thank you for sharing your thoughts and suggestions," and then give yourself some time to think more deeply about it.

❑ **Provide tools and make it engaging**. Help people think outside the box. Reflection questions that are printed out on big chart pages with colorful markers nearby or a whiteboard with sticky notes and soft music playing in the background are all ways to support interactive thinking and creativity.

---

[50] Kolb, DA (1984). *Experiential learning: Experience as the source of learning and development* (Vol. 1). Englewood Cliffs, NJ: Prentice-Hall.

❑ **Record your learnings**. We encourage you to take notes of your reflections. In the future, when your community encounters something similar, you can turn to the documentation and remind yourselves of what you already learned and tried. What might you do differently next time?

Above all, we encourage you to see such learning and reflection as an opportunity to think deeply about what we have accomplished and where we might go next.

This section shares more ideas to help you prepare for unanticipated incidents and put mitigating structures in place, so that you'll feel ready to navigate these uncharted waters with clarity and calmness. By helping to build resilience within the community, it has a better chance of standing the test of time no matter what challenges it may encounter. As you read through the chapters in this section, it may be helpful to hold a specific incident in mind. Can you find ideas or strategies that could offer support to you and your community in this instance?

NOTES

CHAPTER 25
Cultivate an Abundance Mindset

In a strategic planning session with a community I steward, group members began suggesting things that felt way too big for me to hold. I felt my pulse begin to quicken, almost to the point of panic. A website? No time for that! Membership dues? So difficult to manage! In that moment, however, I was able to pause, and notice–aha–this is my scarcity mindset creeping in. I am saying "no" in my heart to these wonderful ideas because I feel like I don't have the time and energy to put them into play. As soon as I recognized that it was my fear of "not enough" saying no, I was able to sit back and listen to all of the ideas without panicking, knowing that the details could be worked out later. —Eva

When a community starts coming together, the possibilities may seem endless. But as we start getting into the day-to-day details of stewarding, coordinating, managing, and operating a community, we may find ourselves in moments where we feel overcome by a sense of doubt, loss of control, competitiveness, or other negative emotions related to scarcity.

Here's what scarcity might sound like:

→ That's impossible. That's never going to work.

→ Are they expecting me to do all that?

→ Why aren't more people showing up?

→ If they try that, they're really going to mess it up.

→ That person has no idea what they are talking about.

We're guessing that you've heard or felt something along these lines at some point of your stewarding journey. By recognizing the source of these feelings, we can choose a different path, rather than letting the feelings of scarcity lead us down a spiral of emotion-driven reactions.

Most feelings of scarcity are based on some arbitrary or unrealistic goals of what it means to have a successful community, including:

→ Our community needs to be getting lots of new members every year.

→ Our budget doesn't allow us to accomplish all of the things we want to achieve.

→ We should host frequent events, and they should all be well-attended.

→ We should be considered the most successful community in our space.

As your mind is spinning on these thoughts of inadequacy, you'll probably feel a physical reaction, like your body tensing up, a twist in your stomach, a sudden feeling of fatigue, or a cold sweat.

If this resonates with you, it may be time to think about how to address a scarcity mindset.

The following tips and ideas are designed to help you shift your thoughts and feelings. While these tips are directed towards you as a Community

Steward, remember that you can also encourage your members to engage in these practices as well. Together, you can address feelings of scarcity and work towards cultivating feelings of abundance instead.

❑ **Practice Mindfulness**. Being honest and authentic about our current state of existence can often be enough to move past difficult thoughts and feelings. As Thich Nhat Hanh has written[51]: "Feelings, whether of compassion or irritation, should be welcomed, recognized, and treated on an absolutely equal basis; because both are ourselves."

Mindfulness encourages practices that help us focus on the present. The first step is to notice when a scarcity mindset is popping up. If we can't notice when it is happening, we can't do anything to address it. What does it feel like in your body when feelings of scarcity arise? Let those feelings arise. You can say to yourself, "Ooooh, I recognize this as my scarcity mindset creeping in. I see you, scarcity!"

If you are experiencing scarcity within a meeting or with other members, pause your meeting and point out, "Hey, I'm noticing some feelings of scarcity here, is anyone else noticing that? Let's examine where this is stemming from." By pausing, we can give ourselves time to try to break out of our old patterns of thinking and doing.

❑ **Revisit your goals**. We often fall into feelings of scarcity when our goals are murky or feel unattainable. Maybe the original ideas for the community were lofty but never clearly stated. Maybe the goals didn't get carried out the way you'd envisioned. Maybe the community's goals never seemed aligned with its mission. Maybe you have too many goals.

There is never a bad time to start over with a new set of goals. Openly discuss the missteps with your community members, and work together to create a new direction.

❑ **Reenvision "failure" as an opportunity to learn and pivot.** If you were hoping to raise $1,000 but only raised $100 through your fundraising, it might be a chance to reposition your efforts into something more accessible to your community. For example, instead of grants, try donations; instead of bake sales, try an auction. What opportunities can you find in this learning moment?

❑ **Avoid Comparisons**. It is so easy to feel let down when it appears that groups around you are flourishing while yours isn't. Instead of comparing your community to others, watch and notice. What are those groups doing? What can you learn from their "success?" Is there a possibility of partnering on activities so you help each other? It also helps to remind yourself that things often look much rosier from the outside than they actually are on the inside.

❑ **Focus on your unique value**. Do you really want to be just like that "other community"? The world is huge, and so is the landscape that your community is a part of. Your community has its own unique value, and there are some things that you are going to be better at than others. Be clear on what value your community offers to the world, and then lean into it.

Part of an abundance mindset is being OK with letting go. Release yourself from feeling like you need to protect what you have. What would it feel like to let go of worrying that if you don't hold it all, things will fall apart?

Our experience is that it feels like a huge relief. Like a weight has been lifted. Like there is now space for more.

Cultivating an abundance mindset can help us be more open-minded about making changes to the ways we steward our communities. As you practice, it will get easier. You'll get better at noticing it, intervening on it, and shifting your perspectives—and those of others around you—away from scarcity and towards abundance. Where can you see scarcity in your community? What can you do to call it out and keep it from snowballing?

---

[51] Hanh, TH (1987). *The Miracle of Mindfulness: a Manual on Meditation.* Boston: Beacon Press.

CHAPTER 26
Assess How Things are Going

> *"How about writing an end-of-the-year report?" one of our community leaders gently suggested. I had never written one before, but it sounded like a good idea to me. I soon realized that it was an exercise of first identifying our community's metrics of success— something that we had never articulated before. I looked through our pages of meeting notes to remember the informal goals that we had set out to accomplish, like developing a new event series, and whether or not we had done it. I added the most obvious quantitative measures like the number of attendees and social media followers, and number of products like blog posts and newsletters. To assess the engagement of our community, I looked towards metrics like community leadership transitions and demographic diversity. I asked all of our most active community members to share what they were most proud of having accomplished, and quoted them in the report so it would reflect different perspectives. Along the way, I asked anyone with responsibilities in the community for ideas of what to include. When it was published—as a simple blog post, we all swelled with pride to see what we had accomplished together. —Arika*

Evaluation is a critical part of community steward-ship, so you can report back to members, funders, a Board or anyone else who is invested in the community to let them know how things are going. It is also a necessary part of continuing to thrive as a community, because without knowing what is currently happening, things could be eroding under your nose without you noticing it.

Many communities avoid evaluation because it can feel overwhelming. To make all of this more manageable, we encourage you to think about evaluation as a continuous effort that occurs through a combination of short-term and long-term cycles.

Short-term evaluation cycles are quick assessments of bite-sized activities like a new event series or a change in a membership application. They support experimentation and improvement in your activities. Table 26.1 provides a basic outline for doing a short term evaluation.

---

[52] The ORID method was developed by the Institute for Cultural Affairs.

Table 26.1. A basic outline for conducting a short-term evaluation cycle.

Evaluation step	Example
Implement a change	→ Start a new event series.
Identify and gather data about the effect of the change	→ Record the number of people that attended each event. → Record the behavior of–and feedback from–people at the events.
Analyze the data	→ Look for patterns in the data, especially those that show differences between events. → Show the information at your next committee meeting, and ask people what they think. → Reflect on your own experiences at the events. → Describe what you learned from the data/doing these events.
Generate iterations	→ Brainstorm other ways you could improve the events.
Decide what to do next	→ Based on analyses, make a change in the events, for example, changing the day of the week that the recurring event occurs. → Use this new change to begin the short-term evaluation cycle again.

A long-term evaluation cycle might look like the end-of-the-year report that Arika shared at the beginning of the chapter, but could also take the form of an organizational evaluation based on your community's multi-year strategic plan. Such larger-scale summaries help us see how we are progressing from year to year, and what we might want to improve. It gives us a chance to step back and see the bigger picture of the community, and to also re-focus our energy on what is most important for the mission of the community itself.

To make these evaluations easier on yourself and the community, look for ways to collect data throughout the year, like recording regular meeting notes or implementing short surveys, so it's easier to aggregate all of this information together in one place when you need to.

There is no one-size-fits-all evaluation approach that works for every community, but to help you scope your evaluation approach better, it can be helpful to consider these four questions:

→ Why are you doing this assessment? (What are your goals?)

→ What questions do you want to answer?

→ What do you want to measure?

→ Who wants to know?

If soliciting input or doing evaluation activities is new to you, it may be beneficial to see if there are any professional evaluators within your community (or consider hiring one) to help guide you through your first full assessment so that you can get the most learning out of it. In addition, your community might benefit from having an outside evaluator provide a less biased perspective than what someone within the community might offer.

Here are some tips to keep in mind as you embark on your assessment journey:

❑ **Maintain an Abundance Mindset.** Feedback that is out of alignment with your own perceptions can be hard to hear. As Community Stewards, we sometimes need to suspend our own judgements and be open to hearing and taking direction from the group. An important step in taking the leap to solicit input is getting yourself internally ready for what might arise, and be willing to listen deeply and let go of anything you've been tightly grasping. Are you ready to learn, even if the learning is difficult?

❑ **Ask for help.** Collecting and making sense of feedback can be a large task. This is an excellent opportunity to form a committee that focuses directly on strategizing and implementing a plan for soliciting input from the community. It also helps to have a designated group or contact so members know where to go when they have a specific piece of feedback they'd like to get off of their chest. Since you'll be evaluating many different things in your community at the same time, for example, an events series, a newsletter template, or a membership application, you may need multiple evaluation teams.

❑ **Include the whole community.** Empower your evaluation team to use a process that is inclusive of everyone. Once the process is initiated, report back anything that the evaluation team finds to the larger community, so that they are fully aware of how the process is going. Create pathways for the community to ask questions or provide feedback on the process.

❑ **Identify ways to collect feedback.** Feedback can be collected in many ways.

Formal methods include:

→ Surveys

→ Focus groups

→ Interviews

→ Suggestions box

Data points might include:

→ Attendance

→ Number of people participating in online conversations

→ Fundraising goals

Less formal formats can consist of:

→ Casual discussions

→ Online dialogues

→ Conversations and observations at an event

When creating your feedback plan, think about what will be easiest for you to manage, as well as what your group members will be able to tap into. A survey might only get a few responses, but you may have many people using the "suggestions" box. The general idea here is to make the process a normal part of your typical workflow, so it's not an extra task that you need to accomplish.

❑ **Consider both qualitative and quantitative feedback.** Think of qualitative feedback as descriptive, and quantitative feedback as numbers-based. Both types of data are important. Quantitative data are generally easier to collect and analyze, while qualitative data may be more time consuming to gather but also more informative.

To make your efforts more manageable, consider collecting quantitative data more frequently and qualitative data less frequently. For example, maybe you collect and analyze event attendance numbers each month (quantitative), and do a survey asking for feedback on an event every other month (qualitative). Taken together, these two types of feedback will provide a robust picture of the success of an event, as it will allow you to compare numbers (how many people attended events) and the quality of attendee experience.

---

[53] To learn about participatory ways to look at data, see: Public Profit (n.d.) *Dabbling in Data: A Hands-on Guide to Participatory Data Analysis.* Public Profit, Oakland CA. https://www.publicprofit.net/dabbling-in-the-data-a-hands-on-guide-to-participatory-data-analysis/

❑ **Make meaning from the data**. Create a plan for how you will use the information that you gather. There are many useful frameworks that you can use to review and analyze data with members of your community[53]. You can ask community members to predict what they think they will see in the data before looking at it. After looking at the data, ask them to compare how their predictions lined up with what was actually in the data–where were they right, and where were they off in their guesses? What were the biggest surprises?

❑ **Be transparent**. When people take the time to share their opinions, they want to know what you did with that information. For example, with survey results, you could share the summarized results with the community on a slide deck or in a newsletter. If you used the feedback that you collected to make changes within your community, then be transparent about that. For example, "95% of the community members that responded to the survey wanted to move our monthly meeting to Tuesday nights, so we are switching the day and time of this event." People like to know that their feedback was valued enough to affect change.

❑ **Respect privacy.** When you collect information from members in a systematic way, such as via a survey, you must always describe up front what the information is going to be used for and who will have access to it (also known as an informed consent). In most cases, survey information is considered private for institutional use only, which means that only admins and analysts have access to the information. However, you can share an aggregate form of the data, such as by showing graphs and statistical summaries that don't reveal the individuals that contributed data. Overall, be very mindful of sharing without consent.

A continuous cycle of evaluation, reflection, and improvement sets up your community to be a "learning organization"[54] that evolves and strengthens its resiliency. By being inclusive and systematic when assessing your community, the whole community can coordinate its learning and move together towards implementing change. Assessments can be an incredible opportunity to inspire and empower your community members towards reaching the shared goals of the community.

NOTES

---

[54] An early use of this term is found in Senge, P (1990) *The Fifth Discipline: The Art and Practice of the Learning Organization*. Penguin Random House.

CHAPTER 27
Address Conflict

It was like watching a train wreck in slow motion. He was making puns about someone in our group's name. Was this actually happening? How could someone be so insensitive? The meeting started, and I kept my eye on him. Afterwards, I quickly consulted a few other members of the group, and we agreed: although we had never explicitly said so to members, this kind of behavior was not at all welcomed in our community. We realized we needed some guidelines, and also that this member needed to be spoken to. After our conversation he ended up deciding to leave the group, and all new members now have to agree to a set of guidelines for interactions that we feel support the kind of environment that benefits our whole community. —Eva

As you read through the chapter, did it bring to mind any parts of your community that might benefit from more focused evaluation? What other suggestions from this chapter might be helpful to your community?

At some point, conflicts will arise within your community. These may be between individual members, or between a member and something that the community as a whole is doing. These conflicts can be explosive, or small but potent, like a bee sting.

The number one piece of advice we can give you is: Do not ignore the conflict, even if you don't know what to do. Conflicts have a pesky inability to resolve themselves. Without intervention, conflicts can snowball very quickly into a destructive force. The truth is, most of us would rather avoid having to deal with a conflict. Confrontation is uncomfortable and stressful, and we often worry that it will flare up even more if we intervene.

To address these fears, we encourage you and your community to create a "conflict plan of action." It can be helpful to think of this plan as having three parts:

1. Prepare for conflict before it happens:

❑ **Develop a process and plan.** Feeling prepared is one of the best ways to alleviate stress. As a steward, make sure that your community has a process for reporting and addressing issues, including providing contact information for whom a community member might reach out to. For many community members, just knowing that there is a way to bring a conflict to the attention of leaders in the community can help reduce the stress and uncertainty that they feel over burbling issues. Include your process in your community handbook so all new members are aware of it.

❑ **Make it easy to talk about conflict.** We might imagine that reporting an incident is a straightforward process where someone recognizes their problem and then reports it to the email address provided. However, the reality is that most people don't immediately jump to "we have a problem." Consider that the people who most often encounter such issues, such as women, people of color, and nonbinary people, are those that have been told repeatedly by society that what they are experiencing is "no big deal." Provide simple–and at least one anonymous way–for members to bring up issues, such as a comment box or online form, and emphasize that all concerns of any shape or size are valid.

❑ **Convene a conflict resolution committee.** Handling conflicts can be a big job, and you don't need to do it all on your own. Identify a pool of people within the community that is willing and able to be part of a conflict resolution committee for when the occasion calls for it. These people may hold leadership roles in the community or are peacemakers skilled in conflict resolution. As you choose people for the committee, make sure you include diverse perspectives, and keep an eye on whether there are biases forming.

If you are facing a truly egregious or sensitive topic, for example a discrimination lawsuit or physical harassment, be aware that you may need to involve third party legal assistance. Your conflict resolution committee can help you decide if this is a route that the community should take.

2. Center yourself in the moment when someone brings a conflict to your attention:

❑ **Take a few minutes.** Conflicts tend to bring out strong emotions from everyone, ranging from defensiveness, to indignation, to sadness. If you find yourself being asked to confront an unexpected conflict, we recommend the following strategies to help you gain strength to address the issue:

→ **Plant your feet on the floor**, notice any sensations or emotions that are arising, be aware of them. A short walk or "shaking it off" physically by moving your body may also be helpful.

→ **Pause.** It is generally best not to address a conflict while you are feeling agitated or upset. If you have the luxury of waiting to reply to the email, take your time. You will likely be able to craft a more coherent

response once you're feeling calm and clear headed.

❑ **Listen to understand.** Active listening is your best tool for addressing conflicts, no matter what process or situation you find yourself in. To actively listen, you need to quiet your natural tendency to respond, judge, or become defensive at whatever is coming towards you. A few strategies to use include:

→ Paraphrase by repeating back what you just heard, to make sure you heard it correctly.

→ Notice non-verbal signals, for example, the person is shaking or has tears in their eyes.

→ Be aware of your body language, for example, uncross your arms, look at the person speaking, and relax your shoulders.

→ Ask questions to gain clarity, such as, when did this happen, why, where?

→ Do not interrupt. Let the person say what they have to say.

→ Feel empathy–can you put yourself in the other person's shoes?

3. Take action:

❑ **Determine if you have a problem.** A member may come to you wondering if they actually have an issue. Practice active listening by staying focused on fully understanding the issue, without jumping to conclusions or responses. To protect yourself from your own biases, it may be helpful to ask your conflict resolution committee to join you. Together as a group, you can refer to previously resolved conflicts and any community policies and values that already exist in order to provide the member with some feedback. Develop and refer members to your appeals process, in case the parties involved want the decision to be re-examined and/or overturned.

❑ **Implement a corrective action.** If you and/or the conflict resolution committee have determined that there is indeed a problem, you'll now have to decide the best way to resolve it. The first thing you'll need to do is ask the person who is being affected about what type of outcome they want. Some conflicts–and especially those where someone is actively being harmed like in Eva's story above–can and should be addressed directly (with the caveat that you and others feel safe doing so). For example, you might ask a leader in the community to reach out to an instigator to tell them to immediately stop what they are doing, while also outlining the boundaries of corrective action and consequences of not staying within those bounds.

Other conflicts may be more subtle and organizational, and can be better tackled in a meeting or series of conversations, like through a restorative justice[55] model, which aims to repair harms through restoring, reconciling, and reintegrating the people involved in a conflict. These processes are an excellent task for your conflict resolution committee to both sift through, and to help lead.

Removing people from the community should be avoided and only done in the most egregious cases. To take this route and avoid legal disputes, you'll need to have specific language in your membership agreement that allows you to take such decisive action. Having a regular membership renewal period is also a helpful way to allow members to gracefully exit a community and offer the community an opportunity to decline a member's renewal.

❑ **Bring in outside help.** If a conflict is too heated or knotty for your community to resolve on its own, you may need to bring in a professional mediator. These are individuals who are trained in how to negotiate conflict and who may be more neutral (and therefore more fair) than anyone from within your community.

Situations that may require outside and/or legal intervention might include:

→ Suspected theft of community assets (including money, intellectual or physical property),

→ Claims or experiences of harassment, assault, or other forms of aggressions,

→ Being sued or threatened by legal action against your community,

→ Other breaches of the law, and

→ Conflicts that you've tried to resolve internally, but keep popping back up.

Just as you've navigated raising funds, developing a governance model, addressing power, and managing other challenging stewardship responsibilities, there are many tools available to help you with both large and small conflicts. Take some time to consider: Which areas of conflict resolution is your community already fluent with? Where do you feel improvements can be made?

---

[55] Menkel-Meadow, C. (2007). Restorative justice: What is it and does it work?. *Annu. Rev. Law Soc. Sci.*, 3(1), 161-187. https://scholarship.law.georgetown.edu/cgi/viewcontent.cgi?article=1588&context=facpub.

NOTES

CHAPTER 28
Honor Privacy

I get really nervous when lists of phone numbers or email addresses get shared around. It is so easy for community members to begin spamming other members, or to reach out with unsolicited questions or offers. We expect people to respect others' boundaries, but they seem to get crossed all of the time. I know I'm not alone when I say that I've got a special email address I use for when I don't trust that my information isn't going to be shared. Wish I could do the same with my phone number so I could reduce the number of spam calls I get every day! —Eva

You've set up all kinds of wonderful ways for members to connect with you, with each other, and with the community as a whole. Relationships are being built, people are reaching out to each other, they're talking, they're supporting each other, the atmosphere is buzzing. Great!

Then, someone feels like another member has overstepped. They've shared confidential information with another member. Worse, they feel like you—as a Community Steward—are not doing enough to protect everyone's private information.

Community Stewards often represent a hub for a group of people, and this includes helping information get passed around more efficiently. On the flip side of that, however, not all information should be shared with everyone, and in every context. What are the different levels of privacy for information within the community? How do you keep information secure? What kind of policies do you need to ensure privacy?

Below are some common situations that you might run across as you are trying to steward your community, and also some ideas about how to deal with each one.

→ **A member who you don't know very well directly shares with you something about their private life.** Sometimes when people join a community, they feel like community leaders are someone they can confide in. What to do with this information?

☐ **Respond to them with empathy** and file this away as a private conversation between you and them. They may even tell you this thing because they perceive that it impacts their ability to participate in the community. In that case, you might want to note something down about the person's membership like "needs a time extension" and leave it at that.

☐ **Communicate your boundaries.** If you sense that the topic is beyond your ability to respond, you can express your concern and suggest that they talk to a professional. With this option, you should be aware of your limitations, and your potential to cause more harm in very sensitive situations.

→ **A member you know well and you enjoy talking with shares private information with you.**

❑ **Treat this like a private conversation between friends** and enjoy the connection. Just because you are the Community Steward doesn't mean that you don't get to have friends too!

→ **Someone accidentally shares a confidential communication with a larger group.** For example, this could look like a community member sharing details about another member's private health issue–without their explicit permission.

❑ **Take immediate action.** Depending on where the information was shared, you may be able to ask the person who posted it to take it down. Otherwise, if the communication is not tractable, you may need to hold a follow up conversation or send another communication with the receiving group to clarify why this information is confidential and why you are asking that it not be shared further.

❑ **Be proactive.** There are a number of preventative measures you can take to reduce the chances you will find yourself in a situation like this, including adding the word "confidential" to documents or communications that you do not want shared, or simply handing all of these types of communications in person so that accidental cc's or document sharing cannot happen.

→ **A member has a concern about another member.**

❑ **Invoke your conflict resolution process.** Any conflict between two members that is brought to your attention should be treated as highly sensitive information. If the member just wants to express a concern and get your personal advice on something, then keep that information strictly to yourself unless the member asks for the next steps in the conflict resolution process to be taken.

→ **A member shares information via a form or other systematic data collection mode.**

❑ **Be intentional with surveys.** Make sure you have informed consent for any data you are collecting from members.

❑ **Be clear on the ownership of data.** Consider the high standards of the EU's General Data Protection Regulation (GDPR, https://gdpr-info.eu) and match these rules in any data collection you engage in. In other words, everyone has the right to remove information about themselves.

❑ **Don't collect personal information that you don't need.** Sometimes we get in the habit of collecting information that we assume is needed. For example, perhaps it's a standard question on a newsletter sign-up form, and you didn't think about removing it. Before you collect people's information, consider: How important is this information for the purposes of the community? Do we really need to know every member's mailing address and phone number? If not, then don't collect it. Otherwise, you're creating more work for yourself by needing to caretake the information. Similarly, your community should be honest with itself about its own capability to protect such private data.

Take a moment to reflect on how you currently handle privacy issues in your community. Do you have any shared agreements or processes related to privacy? Are there any current situations around privacy that you feel need to be addressed? If this is a topic that keeps cropping up, we encourage you to bring it up with your community so you can examine it and take action together.

CHAPTER 29
Integrate the Concept of Wellness

"Just letting you know that my little son is around. He's home sick." As a work-from-home parent, I have said this more times than I can count this past winter while getting on a video call, anticipating when my sick child might pop into the video, call out for me, or worse–start throwing up again. When my kids are sick, it's like being sick myself, staying up all night to help them to the bathroom and worrying at every hacking cough and rattling breath. Nothing like a sleepless stressful night to make it tough for me to show up to anything the next day. —Arika

How many times have you gone to work not feeling like your best self while juggling grief, illness, or hardship and felt the pressure to plow through your day like nothing else is going in your life?

Communities emerge at the pace of life. When life and the world intervene unexpectedly, we find our need to be present in the community competing with our need to tend to ourselves.

Ignoring our bodies, our emotions, and our personal needs often results in resentment and distancing–eventually leading to burnout. Incorporating elements of "wellness" into communities helps members feel supported and cared for as individuals, instead of as disposable worker bees where the goals of the community come first.

In order to move towards being a kinder, more human-centered entity, we encourage you to build collective care and wellness into the central vision for your community. Here are some ideas for how to do this:

❑ **Develop norms that include activities that attend to the body, mind, and heart**. As you develop expectations for your community, include explicit norms or activities that focus on whole-human wellness. For example, lead a moment of pause for three deep breaths before launching into a conversation. Your community can also plan and engage in on-going physical or social events (e.g., weekly walks, monthly outings), as well as commit to having healthy snacks and hydration at events.

Another option is to create a "wellness response team" that attends to members' life events and organizes care activities when a member needs additional support. Activities of the team could include sending flowers, coordinating meal-trains, and checking in with members. An important part of this approach is to create a way for the team to be notified when/if a member needs support. Is there an online form? A specific point person? This team can also create a protocol for how to respond to various needs, and offer those members a menu of options if the situation arises.

❑ **Use trauma-informed practices**. Originally developed to support veterans returning from the Vietnam War, trauma-informed care is designed to foster resilience in individuals and groups who have experienced extreme distress. Over the past fifty years, the practices have been successfully implemented in a wide range of community settings, and are an excellent way to promote wellness within your group. There are varying frameworks, but most fall somewhere into these categories:

→ Safety: Do your members feel safe within your community?

→ Choice: Do your members feel like they have control over decisions?

→ Collaboration: Do members have opportunities to work together?

→ Trustworthiness: Do members trust each other? Do they trust you?

→ Empowerment: Do members have opportunities to lead and take control?

Take a moment to reflect on how you currently cultivate these practices in your community.

❑ **Use a rubric so wellness is centered in all you do**. A rubric is simply a way to measure how well you are doing in your quest to meet specific goals. It requires that you name and write down what those goals are and then either give yourself a score rating, or judge whether you are "not yet started," "in process," or "completed" in your progress towards reaching those goals.

Some of your wellness goals might include:

→ We know and respond when someone in our community is going through a hard time.

→ In meetings and conversations, we pause and acknowledge when members are experiencing grief or strife.

→ We intentionally create time/space for wellness and healing.

❑ **Don't take it personally.** People need time and space to heal and process from events that might be happening around them. For our community work, this means accepting when people don't show up in the ways that you might expect or want them to. Keep in mind that you often only see the tip of an iceberg, or just a small slice of their life, when you interact with someone.

When a member says they need to keep their camera off during the group video call, reschedule a meeting, or step back from an activity altogether, you might initially feel a twinge of annoyance or disappointment. If you notice those feelings coming up for you, acknowledge them, and let them go. Remind yourself of the bigger picture, and reach for care instead. You could respond with, "Thanks for letting me know. Please take care of yourself. Whenever you are ready to join the planning group again, we'll love to have you back."

Create an expectation and a culture that nurtures a guilt-free space where people feel comfortable acknowledging their limitations and boundaries. You might, for example, start the routine of regular check-in's at the start of a group meeting or once a week for a team, where someone might acknowledge: "I'm feeling really overwhelmed today." Making space, in the long run, will allow people to be their best selves when they *are* present.

❑ **Create teams, so tasks do not fall on one individual**. As you help design the roles and responsibilities of community members, work towards building teams that can collectively shoulder projects or assignments, so that if a member needs to take a pause, they can do so easily, without causing disruption to the overall community.

Wellness in your community may feel like a luxury or a nice-to-have, but putting it first will help you maintain a cohesive group that feels heard, cared for, and centered. It will very likely help *you* feel that way, too. As you read through this chapter, which ideas felt new or refreshing to you? That may be the best place to start!

CHAPTER 30
Know When It's Time to Wrap Up or Reform

I was stewarding a community that had a strong value of social equity, when I began to suspect that our community demographics were beginning to lean more male than in the past. I started making counts of things that I saw—like the composition of new membership, leadership, speakers, and volunteers. This exploratory information was enough to convince other leaders in the community to do a more formalized demographic analysis, and we were able to definitively conclude that our community had been quickly becoming more male over the last few years.

Having identified what we viewed as a problem, we started brainstorming about why it was happening and what we should do. We came up with multiple solutions to try, but one that I was really proud of was our new policy that all prospective members had to attend one community event (all online) before being able to submit an application for membership. Later, we learned that there was a name for the behavior that we were looking for: "congressive" (versus "ingressive"), which basically means being community-minded, as articulated so eloquently in Eugenia Cheng's book on gender equity[56]. This one policy began to quickly get our demographics more balanced, and importantly, also greatly improved the quality of our membership—people who joined were more interested in actively participating in the community, regardless of their gender. —Arika

Communities evolve over time—whether you want them to or not. Resisting change can feel like it is strengthening your position, but recognizing when it's time to change or end something is key to being able to guide the direction a community goes in and ensure longevity.

Because impending change can be disorienting and feel like you are on unstable ground, we've assembled some suggestions for how to navigate the inevitable.

❑ **Assume that everything you create in a community is temporary.** This means your policies, processes, leadership, and other key components of your community are fluid. Some elements will last longer than others, like your mission, values, and culture, but even these may evolve. Assuming that change is inevitable means that you can plan for it, for example, by creating documents that are easy to change and update, doing succession planning, or

---

[56] Cheng, E. (2020). *X+ Y: A Mathematician's Manifesto for Rethinking Gender.* Hachette UK.

scheduling annual meetings to revisit key areas of your strategy.

❑ **Recognize when it's time to change.** It could be that something just isn't going as expected or your community has an activity that no longer fits with your values and mission. Communities are not perfect, and there is always room for improvement. Keep your mind and ears open and listen to community members when they tip you off, either with words or actions, that change is needed. Once you've gotten the signals, ask around to confirm your hunch that it's time to pivot and begin working on a plan.

❑ **Know when it's time to end.** It's also OK to end parts of your community. If you've got an event series where attendance has really started to drop–and importantly, whomever has been leading it doesn't feel like pushing it forward anymore, then by all means, quit. If there is a volunteer role that no one is stepping up to do, consider how important it is to the functioning of the community. If it's really important, that's when a community manager (or paid staff) steps in. If it's not that important, then put it on the back burner. Don't keep an activity (or even a community) going for the sake of doing it.

❑ **Know the difference between a minor vs. major pivot.** While minor pivots might be able to be easily done based on the decision and actions of a few people, major pivots require bringing the community along in the process. Introducing a big change in a community is best approached like "a slow turning of the ship," the bigger the turn, the slower and more consistent the speed. This helps members adjust to the changes, and helps you see how it's going so you can make sure that you are staying on course.

A minor pivot are things that affect a one-off event or a limited number of people, or are already planned as part of an existing process. Here are some examples:

→ Canceling or changing the time of an event

→ Changing an online platform used by a few people in the community (like accounting software)

→ Changing or introducing new people into existing roles

A major pivot has systemic implications for the community, affects everyone who is a part of the community, and may run counter to members' existing expectations. Here are some examples:

→ Changing the business model, like introducing membership fees

→ Introducing new rules for membership, such as a policy change

→ Changing or introducing a new top-level mission or value

→ Changing an online platform that many members use

Because major pivots are likely to cause more waves than minor pivots, here are a few suggestions for how to introduce a major pivot, although the ideas also work for smaller changes as well:

❑ **Start by talking to a few core trusted members to see what they think.** Together, you can brainstorm and consider all possibilities, including asking the 5 Whys[57] to consider why the change is needed. You'll also need to get their feedback on any anticipated risks of the change. Make sure to ask yourselves what might happen if you made no change at all.

❑ **Find your allies.** Your position within the community and/or your identity may affect your ability to move things along because of both the public perception of your interest in the shift, and because of traditional power dynamics. Building a multi-dimensional team of champions for the change can help motivate broader support across a diversity of members.

---

[57] See details about the 5 Whys tool in Chapter 4 on Notice who's missing.

❑ **Communicate the change broadly–and listen.** Provide different venues for people to learn about the proposed change and voice their concerns and opinions. In these events, make sure that you do more listening than talking.

❑ **Make the change in increments, if possible.** Slow and steady is the guidance here. Consider how intermediary steps might help you alter the subsequent steps and lead you to the end goal of bringing everyone along for the change peacefully.

Guiding a major change in a community is one of the most fulfilling parts of being a Community Steward. It means that you've managed to bring everyone on board with you, as you've steered the community towards a new direction and future.

Stepping away from stewardship or passing the baton to someone else can be a very difficult decision, but whatever you decide to do, all of the suggestions in this chapter still apply–take it slow, communicate, and work in community so that people feel they have options for what will happen next. Being able to let go of a community as it continues its journey also means that you understand what it truly means to be a "Community Steward".

NOTES

Afterword

"Do you remember that time in Laos when we stayed in that village and there was nothing to eat but snails, sticky rice, and cucumbers?" That was one of the first things that Eva and I said to each other when we reconnected after 20 years. We had first met years ago when we were both carrying out research as Fulbright Scholars in Thailand. At that time, Eva was based in Bangkok working with educators and I was located in a rural Thai town about six hours away studying Thai ethnobiology. It was a delight to discover that we had come full circle. We shared similar interests and philosophies in community building—both believing in a participant-centered approach. It wasn't long before we began the conversation about what it might look like to write a book together. What would happen if we combined my wisdom from my years of working with place-based communities and "Community Activation[58]," and Eva's skills of facilitating communities within the nonprofit and education sectors? Was there enough overlap within those circles to make a case for the importance of writing a guide for Community Stewards? The resounding answer was "yes." —Arika

We hope that as you've read this guide, you've gotten a deeper understanding of what it means to be a Community Steward. Perhaps, like us, you found your own thoughts changing and growing along the way.

To check in with yourself, you could head back to those pre-assessments you started out with at the beginning of the guide to see what may have changed for you. Are there parts of your community that you feel especially proud of? What are some things that you might still want to work on?

We realize that change in communities—and in ourselves—is slow. It takes time, reflection, and iteration to find the balance and solutions that are best for your community and you. Sometimes, what may be right for one moment, may not be best for the next.

This complexity is something that we love about community stewardship. You never quite know what you're getting into, or where you're going. But nonetheless, it feels so fulfilling.

Some time in the future, after your community has evolved a little more, come back and flip through this guide again. What new ideas stand out to you now? What have you learned?

It was a multi-year adventure for us to write this guide, and in that time so much changed for us—in our careers, our lives, and in the world. As we mused and shared with each other our thoughts around community stewardship, our ideas for the

---

[58] Virapongse, A. (2025). Community Activation: What is it?. Middle Path EcoSolutions. https://doi.org/10.5281/zenodo.15238155

book changed too. There were many times when we re-wrote a chapter because we felt that we had learned and grown beyond it, until finally it felt just right.

One day, while discussing the title, we discovered that we were writing not a book, but a guide. Something that our readers could take along with them as a companion on their own travels through community stewardship. Something to help them feel like they were not alone, but that everyone doing the work was there alongside them. Something that helped them see that there was a path of transformation happening–from Me to We.

Like community stewardship, writing a guide is a process of growth. We expect that reading it is too. To us, this guide represents just part of our journey as Community Stewards. The remainder of the journey has yet to be written, but we hope that by sharing our thoughts with you all, we can write that part together.

NOTES

Acknowledgements

We would like to thank all of the people who helped to review and provide comments on earlier drafts of the book, including Emily Monosson, John Paulas, Morgan Shidler, Megan Wells, Keith Tse, Oscar Wolters-Duran, Masumi Hayashi-Smith, Sharon Ng, and contributors via our LinkedIn page. Your feedback made this book exponentially better.

Our thinking for this book was greatly shaped by the different communities that we've had the honor to be a part of and contribute towards. Thank you all so much for your time and wisdom!

Financial support to bring this to life was provided by Spark Decks, LLC and Middle Path EcoSolutions, LLC.

NOTES

Stay Connected

If you have thoughts on Community Stewardship and on this book, please share them with us via our LinkedIn page, or our websites www.evajomeyers.com, spark-decks.com, and Middle Path EcoSolutions www.middlepatheco.com. Reviews for our guide are also greatly appreciated via the same links, or anywhere that you purchase books.

NOTES

Bibliography

Aral, S. (2016). The future of weak ties. *American Journal of Sociology, 121*(6), 1931–1939.

Associated Press. (2025, April 16). Book brigade: US town forms human chain to move 9,100 books one-by-one. *The Guardian.* www.theguardian.com

Boal, A. (1974). *Theater of the oppressed.* Ediciones de la Flor.

Boal, A. (1992). *Games for actors and non-actors.* Routledge.

Bollier, D., & Helfrich, S. (2019). *Free, fair, and alive: The insurgent power of the commons.* New Society Publishers. freefairandalive.org

brown, a. m. (2017). *Emergent strategy.* AK Press.

Cain, S. (2012). *Quiet: The power of introverts in a world that can't stop talking.* Crown.

Cheng, E. (2020). *X + Y: A mathematician's manifesto for rethinking gender.* Hachette UK.

CommunityWiki. (n.d.). *DoOcracy.* communitywiki.org

Freire, P. (1970). *Pedagogy of the oppressed.* Seabury Press.

Gray, P. (2013). *Free to learn: Why unleashing the instinct to play will make our children happier, more self-reliant, and better students for life.* Basic Books.

Hanh, T. N. (1987). *The miracle of mindfulness: A manual on meditation.* Beacon Press.

Hou, X., Li, R., & Song, Z. (2022). A bibliometric analysis of wicked problems: From single discipline to transdisciplinarity. *Fudan Journal of the Humanities and Social Sciences, 15*(3), 299–329. https://doi.org/10.1007/s40647-022-00346-w

International Cooperative Alliance. (n.d.). *Cooperative identity, values & principles.* ica.coop

Kador, T., & Chatterjee, H. (Eds.). (2020). *Object-based learning and well-being: Exploring material connections.* Routledge.

Kolb, D. A. (1984). *Experiential learning: Experience as the source of learning and development* (Vol. 1). Prentice-Hall.

Kondo, M. (2014). *The life-changing magic of tidying: A simple, effective way to banish clutter forever.* Random House.

Laudel, G., & Gläser, J. (2008). From apprentice to colleague: The metamorphosis of early career researchers. *Higher Education, 55,* 387–406. https://doi.org/10.1007/s10734-007-9063-7

Lave, J., & Wenger, E. (2001). Legitimate peripheral participation in communities of practice. In *Supporting lifelong learning* (pp. 121–136). Routledge.

Lego. (n.d.). *Serious Play.* www.lego.com

Menakem, R. (2017). *My grandmother's hands: Racialized trauma and the pathway to mending our hearts and bodies.* Central Recovery Press.

Menkel-Meadow, C. (2007). Restorative justice: What is it and does it work? *Annual Review of Law and Social Science, 3*(1), 161–187.

Meta & Gallup. (2023). *The global state of social connections.* Gallup Inc. www.gallup.com

Meyers, E. J. (2019). *Raise the room: A practical guide to participant-centered facilitation.* Spark Decks.

Mizelle, S. (2022, December 7). Arkansas city elects 18-year-old to be next mayor. *CNN.* www.cnn.com

Murthy, V. H. (2020). *Together: The healing power of human connection in a sometimes lonely world*. HarperCollins.

National Academies of Sciences, Engineering, and Medicine. (2025). *The science and practice of team science*. The National Academies Press. https://doi.org/10.17226/29043

Oldenburg, R. (1989). *The great good place: Cafes, coffee shops, bookstores, bars, hair salons, and other hangouts at the heart of a community*. Da Capo Press.

Ostrom, E. (1990). *Governing the commons: The evolution of institutions for collective action*. Cambridge University Press.

Parker, P. (2020). *The art of gathering: How we meet and why it matters*. Penguin.

Public Profit. (n.d.). *Dabbling in data: A hands-on guide to participatory data analysis*. Public Profit.

Rau, T. (2022). *Consent decision making*. Sociocracy For All. www.sociocracyforall.org

Robert, H. M., III, Honemann, D. H., Balch, T. J., Seabold, D. E., & Gerber, S. (2020). *Robert's rules of order newly revised*. PublicAffairs.

Salas, J., & Fox, J. (n.d.). *International Playback Theatre Network*. https://www.playback-centre.org

Sandfort, J., Stuber, N., & Quick, K. (2012). *Practicing the Art of Hosting*. University of Minnesota.

Scharmer, C. O. (2009). *Theory U: Learning from the future as it emerges*. Berrett-Koehler Publishers.

Senge, P. M. (1990). *The fifth discipline: The art and practice of the learning organization*. Penguin Random House.

Serrat, O. D. (2009). *The five whys technique*. Asian Development Bank. www.adb.org

Sociocracy for All. (2023). *Sociocracy vs Holacracy: What are the similarities and differences between them?*. www.sociocracyforall.org

Spradley, J. P. (1979). *The ethnographic interview*. Waveland Press.

State Support Network. (2019). *Problems of practice toolkit: Action planning for rural schools and districts*. Office of Elementary and Secondary Education. oese.ed.gov

Virapongse, A. (2025). *Community activation: What is it?*. Middle Path EcoSolutions. https://doi.org/10.5281/zenodo.15238155

Virapongse, A., Gallagher, J., & Tikoff, B. (2024). Insights on sustainability of Earth Science data infrastructure projects. *Data Science Journal*, *23*(14), 1–27. https://doi.org/10.5334/dsj-2024-014

Virapongse, A., Gupta, R., Robbins, Z., Blythe, J., Duerr, R., & Gregg, C. (2022). How can Earth scientists contribute to community resilience? Challenges and recommendations. *Frontiers in Climate*. https://doi.org/10.3389/fclim.2022.761499

World Bank. (2023). *The world by income and region*. datatopics.worldbank.org

About the Authors

Eva Jo Meyers, M.A.
Eva has a Bachelor's degree in Visual Art and Community Activism from Oberlin College, a Master's Degree in Humanities and Leader-ship from New College of California, and earned her CA Teaching Credential in Art from San Francisco State University. She was a Fulbright scholar in Thailand from 1999-2000 studying the impact of culture on pedagogy. Eva has published numerous articles on topics related to education, equity, and facilitation in periodicals including FastCompany, Afterschool Today Magazine, and Parents.com. Her first book, "Raise the Room: A practical guide to participant-centered facilitation," was published in 2019. Eva is the co-founder and owner of Spark Decks, a publishing company that supports professional development for change-makers (www.spark-decks.com). She has taught and run youth programs in New York, San Francisco, Bangkok (Thailand), Chongqing (China), and Ako (Japan) and currently spends her days facilitating workshops and retreats for school districts, government agencies, and nonprofits throughout California and the U.S.

Arika Virapongse, M.S., Ph.D.
Arika's academic interests have taken her from fine art and ethnobotany to traditional medicine and natural resource manage-ment and to community science. She has spent years learning about how people and communities live with their local natural environment in Thailand as a Fulbright scholar, on the eastern coast and the Amazon of Brazil, and in many other places in the world. Today, as a scholar and consultant based in Boulder, Colorado, Arika focuses her work on social-ecological resilience and community-based systems. She's published dozens of scientific and public-facing articles, and is often called upon by organizations to help develop their community engagement strategies. As dedicated world schoolers, Arika and her family spend as much time as they can practicing place-based learning. Any chance she gets, you can find Arika snowboarding, perusing library books, growing vegetables, and riding her bike around town. Learn more about Arika here: www.middlepatheco.com